BROADER
than
beans

BROADER
than
beans

Lesley Waters

with photographs by Gus Filgate

HEADLINE

for Tim and Isaac
the two men in my life

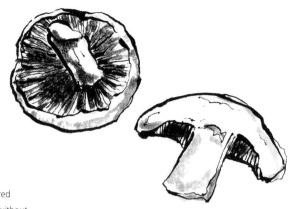

First published in 1998
by HEADLINE BOOK PUBLISHING

10 9 8 7 6 5 4 3 2 1

British Library Cataloguing in Publication Data is available from the British Library
    ISBN 0 7472 2163 4

Frontispiece: Thai Broth with Crispy Noodles (see page 72)
Page 7: Sticky Coconut Rice with Caramelised Spicy Fruits (see pages 136 and 137)

Typeset by Letterpart Limited, Reigate, Surrey
Designed by Isobel Gillan
Illustrations by Alison Jeffrey
Printed and bound in Italy by Canale & C.S.p.A

HEADLINE BOOK PUBLISHING
    A division of Hodder Headline PLC
    338 Euston Road
    London NW1 3BH

Acknowledgements

My very special thanks go to Louise Wooldridge for all her hard work on the book and her unfaltering encouragement and patience throughout. I am also grateful to Fiona Lindsay and Heather Holden-Brown for their enthusiasm and sound advice, and to my editor Susan Fleming for all her help, guidance and wisdom.

Thanks to Gus Filgate and Maxine Clark for their inspired photography. Finally, I would like to thank all the cooks, family and friends who have inspired and taught me over the years, Annalisa for allocating a few days, and Tim and Jim for always being devoted tasters with insatiable appetites.

> ⓥ **This symbol, which appears at the bottom of some recipes, indicates where meat or fish can be added to a dish.**

Contents

Introduction

Not so long ago an everyday main meal would always include meat. Vegetables were very much second-class citizens, not important enough even to be referred to individually. How our tastes have changed! The modern way of eating is combining good fresh ingredients – and often the majority of these are vegetables – to create masses of flavour and a healthier diet. Roast some vegetables, wok up a stir-fry, nosh out on noodles or toss in some pasta – the name of the game is quick and simple, and for much of the time, meat is used only as a flavouring or even left out completely. Vegetables and meatless dishes have at long last taken a much deserved leading role.

Nowadays, nearly half of the UK population (46 per cent) say they eat less meat than they used to. In fact Britain has the greatest number of veggies in Europe. According to the Vegetarian Society, 5,000 people every week give up meat. Maybe this is hardly surprising when, according to a study at Edinburgh University, veggies have a more robust sex life!

Vegetarian or not, *Broader Than Beans* is the modern approach. The recipes are meatless, but will appeal to all. They represent an explosion of flavours from all over the world, mixed and matched, often with more than one country inspiring a single dish.

From the word go, the foundations are laid for great cooking. There are recipes for adding an extra kick to your food, from simple flavoured oils to zingy stocks, salsas and sauces. Other chapters range from nibbles and tapas, for light, quick home or party eating, to cooking up a spread for more than just the family. What lies in between is a collection of vegetarian dishes to thrill and excite all appetites and tastes. *Broader Than Beans* is a cookery book for everyone, and it can and should be used every day. There are no rules or regulations; simply enjoy these dishes at any time, and at every opportunity!

My original title for the book was *Pleasures Without the Flesh*. At the time I really felt this was the perfect title: it was a play on words, clever and funny, and I thought it neatly summed up how you could eat really good food without meat. Now I'm glad that I changed my mind. While writing and cooking these recipes – and I must tell you that I am not a vegetarian myself – I realised that it's not about eating without meat, it's simply about great-tasting, healthier food for everyone.

A WORD ON HEALTH

Not eating meat doesn't guarantee a healthy diet. As a non-meat eater, it is perhaps even more necessary to ensure that your body receives the right fuel in the right balance. Variety is the key, and a nutritious non-meat diet should include a good mix.

Here are a few tips to guide you:
● Spend a little time on planning your meals. The best diets include the whole range of foods, and include carbohydrates, vitamins, minerals, fats and proteins.
● Carbohydrates include sugar and starches. Try to avoid sugar and sugary foods, and instead eat breads (preferably brown), cereals (avoiding refined cereals), potatoes and other vegetables and fruit.
● The vitamins and minerals essential for the body are contained in fresh and natural, preferably raw, foods. They are low in refined or processed foods.
● Fats come from both vegetable and animal sources. Those from seeds, nuts, grains and vegetable oils are more valuable than those from animal sources (meat, oily fish and dairy products).
● 'Complete' proteins are provided by meat, fish, dairy products, eggs and soya beans (the only vegetable food which is a complete protein). 'Incomplete' proteins are provided by nuts, seeds, peas, beans, lentils, whole grains and brown rice. Vegetarians should therefore combine different types of vegetable protein for an adequate intake and balance of protein – rice with pulses, wheat with pulses or nuts, nuts with seeds, etc. The addition of eggs, milk, yoghurt or cheese increases the protein content and nutrition of vegetarian dishes.

● It's well known, however, that dairy products can feature too heavily in a vegetarian diet, so don't let your protein, thus fat, intake creep up. Try to get most of your protein from other sources already mentioned and, of course, if you like it, tofu (a soya bean product).
● Nuts and seeds are a source of protein, carbohydrate and fat. Use them in salads or sprinkled in sandwiches. Try sprouted seeds (and sprouted pulses and grains) in salads as well; they are rich in Vitamin C.
● Don't throw away vegetable cooking water, as it contains goodness and flavour. Use it as stock in sauces and soups.
● The body must be well watered to function well. Drink plenty of water and fresh fruit and vegetable juices.
● Skipping meals can easily lead to an unhealthy diet, especially if you buy ready-made snack foods. These foods can be high in fat, sugar and salt.
● Make time for your meals and, most importantly, relax when you eat so that you can enjoy your food fully.

Bare Essentials
To cook food you don't need a vast array of gadgets or a huge kitchen. However, there are some pieces of equipment used in these recipes that will make your life easier.

Food processor
A simple food processor for blitzing food quickly.

Mini food processor
Inexpensive and brilliant for pastes, pestos or any small amount of food that disappears in a large processor.

Pestle and mortar

For freshly grinding your spices, a pestle and mortar is invaluable.

Sharp knives

Little and large, the investment is well worth it. You should have a small *sharp* vegetable knife and a large *sharp* chopping knife. *Keep* them sharp!

Wok

One of the most versatile large pans in the kitchen. Don't just use it for stir-fries, but try it too for steaming, deep-frying, and for soups. I couldn't exist without mine.

Heavy-based frying pan

Invest in a good one and, if possible, one that transfers straight to the oven.

What's in Store

A storecupboard may sound like a thing of the past, but the modern version can be a treasure-chest of fabulous staples, spices and flavourings which, combined with the new deli-style ingredients, means that stylish and innovative dishes can be created quickly at any time.

So, get tough. Organise your storecupboard so that your stores – jars, tins, flavourings and spices etc. – all have their own space, and throw away any that are past it! This makes it easier for quick stock-checks before a shopping trip, and prevents wasting time rummaging through every cupboard to look for that important ingredient.

Don't forget the twentieth-century storecupboards, the fridge and freezer. Divide your fridge into the appropriate sections – e.g. dairy, cooked, uncooked and salad items. Once again this makes life a lot easier for that last-minute spot-check.

The Ten Essentials

Rice – long-grain, basmati, Thai fragrant, risotto, easy-cook brown

Beans and Lentils – (canned or dried) orange and green lentils, Puy lentils, chickpeas, borlotti beans, cannellini beans, butter beans, broad beans

Grains and Flours – pearl barley, bulgar wheat, polenta, porridge oats, couscous, plain, self-raising and granary flours

Dried Pasta and Noodles – egg pasta, spinach pasta, egg noodles, rice noodles

Sun-dried and Antipasto Vegetables (the latter in jars) – tomatoes, aubergines, chillies, mushrooms, peppers, artichokes, onions

Nuts and Seeds – walnuts, almonds, hazelnuts, pine kernels, cashew nuts, coconut, chestnuts, pecan nuts, sesame seeds, poppy seeds

Oils and Vinegars – virgin olive oil, walnut oil, sesame oil, grapeseed oil, sunflower oil, white wine vinegar, red wine vinegar, balsamic vinegar, raspberry vinegar, cider vinegar

Dried Fruits – apricots, prunes, sultanas, figs, dates, raisins

Whole Spices – black and white peppercorns, cinnamon sticks, whole nutmeg, coriander seeds, cumin seeds, green cardamom pods, kaffir lime leaves, bay leaves, vanilla pods, star anise, cloves

Sauces, Pastes and Flavourings – light and dark soy sauces, runny honey, maple syrup, red and green Tabasco sauces, chilli sauce, black bean sauce, sun-dried tomato paste, Dijon and grainy mustards, horseradish sauce, curry paste, canned plum, chopped and cherry tomatoes, tomato passata, olive pastes

Infusions and ESSENTIALS

Although the recipes in this chapter are not in fact complete dishes in themselves, they provide you with important bases (such as marinades or stocks) and accompaniments (such as instant salsas, relishes and chutneys) that will enhance your daily dishes and give them that special edge.

Most of these recipes would appear at the back of other cookery books, but I have placed them at the beginning of mine, because they are so much to the forefront of *taste*. A simple dish of steamed vegetables becomes something sublime when spiked with an infused oil; a baked potato or bowl of buttery pasta is transformed by some baked tomato chutney . . . These simple, no-fuss recipes are quick, practical, modern and entirely relevant to the recipes that follow in the rest of the book.

INFUSED OILS

There is a lot of culinary hype surrounding oils these days, and the choice can be bewildering. Does oil have to be expensive to be good? And does each oil have a specific use?

For me, at the end of the day, it's really all a matter of personal taste. If I had to choose, my personal favourite is olive oil, in whatever form. But sunflower, soya and grapeseed are useful as base and cooking oils, and walnut, sesame and hazelnut are all ideal for instant flashes of flavour.

Cold-pressed or virgin olive oils come usually from the first pressing of the olives, and are therefore purer. Although these oils are the most expensive, they are intense in flavour, so a little goes a long way. Being unrefined, they do not store for long, and are best bought in small quantities. Keep away from heat and light, and the lid should be kept tightly on. Not really for cooking with, these oils are at their best added to cooked food as a final flourish, or as a dressing on cold (or warm) food.

High-quality oils are now also available infused with herbs and spices. Once again they can be expensive, but are easily made up at home in whatever quantity you require. Oils can be flavoured with chillies, whole spices, garlic, ginger, lemongrass, citrus peel and herbs. Use the blander oils such as sunflower, soya or grapeseed.

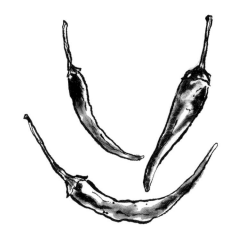

The Instant Pan Infusion

Gently heat the required amount of oil in the cooking pan with the desired flavouring for 2–3 minutes. Lift out the flavouring and continue your chosen recipe. For instance, a big dried red chilli and a thick slice of bruised ginger work well. You could add a garlic clove too.

The Cold Infusion

Mix your chosen oil and flavouring in a thoroughly clean container with a tight-fitting lid. Keep in a cool place and use within two weeks. About 3 fat cloves of garlic to 300ml (10 fl oz) olive oil would be lovely – great for trickling over warm crusty bread or tossing through some pasta.

The Heat Infusion

For a more intense flavour, very gently heat your chosen oil with your chosen flavourings for 1 minute, before cooling and storing in a thoroughly clean container with a tight-fitting lid. Keep in a cool place and use within two weeks. This would work well with a large piece of lemon rind and a couple of sprigs of fresh thyme.

SALSAS, RELISHES AND CHUTNEYS

Here are some no-fuss recipes which you can whip up in no time. Use them as partners to a range of staples such as pasta, polenta, couscous or rice, and serve them as a tasty topping for a baked potato, or to liven up a sandwich or your cheeseboard. Use some of them as dips with breads, corn chips, crisps, breadsticks or crudités. And, of course, they're great served with curries . . .

Mango and Mint Raita

Serve with Spicy Rice and Beans (see page 76), or any curry dish.

Serves 4

280g (10 oz) natural yoghurt
3 tablespoons mango chutney
1 bunch of fresh mint leaves
salt and black pepper

1 In a liquidiser, whizz together the yoghurt, mango chutney and mint leaves.
2 Season to taste.

Date and Coriander Raita

This raita is very good with lentil dishes or any curry (see the photograph on page 82).

Serves 4–6

115g (4 oz) dates, chopped
2 tablespoons roughly chopped fresh coriander
280g (10 oz) natural or Greek-style yoghurt
2 spring onions, chopped
salt and black pepper

1 Simply combine all the raita ingredients in a bowl, and pour into a serving dish.
2 Chill for 30 minutes before serving.

Red Onion and Coriander Salsa

This salad style relish is really refreshing and full of taste.
It's very good served with the Puy lentils on page 84.

Serves 4

1 small red onion, finely sliced
1 bunch of fresh coriander

For the dressing (optional):
2 tablespoons olive oil
a squeeze of lime juice
salt and black pepper

1 Combine the red onion with the coriander leaves.
2 Toss with the olive oil if required and season to taste with the lime juice, salt and pepper.

Raw Tomato Salsa

Great as a pizza topping, on potatoes, pasta or polenta,
or as a dip with tortilla chips.

Serves 4, depending on use

1 large red pepper, de-seeded and diced
4 ripe tomatoes, diced
2 spring onions, finely chopped
1 tablespoon virgin olive oil
a pinch of sugar
a squeeze of lemon juice
1 garlic clove, crushed (optional)
Tabasco sauce to taste
salt and black pepper

1 In a bowl, combine all the salsa ingredients together, adding Tabasco meagrely or 'generously' depending on the heat you like.
2 Season well and set to one side.

Pineapple and Roasted Sweetcorn Salsa

Serve with Pan-fried Halloumi Cheese (see page 40).

Serves 4

1 large corn on the cob
1 teaspoon olive oil
salt and black pepper
½ medium pineapple, peeled, cored and diced
½ small red onion, diced
1 red chilli, de-seeded and finely chopped
1 fresh green chilli, de-seeded and finely chopped
2 tablespoons virgin olive oil
juice of ½ lime

1 Preheat the oven to 220°C/425°F/Gas Mark 7.
2 Brush the corn on the cob with the olive oil, and season with salt and pepper. Bake in the preheated oven for 20–25 minutes until the corn is just cooked and beginning to brown.
3 When the corn is cooked, allow to cool slightly. Remove the kernels from the cob with a sharp knife.
4 Combine in a bowl with all the other salsa ingredients. Season and set to one side.

Cranberry Salsa

This keeps for several days in the fridge. It's fabulous with Stilton cheese, or on top of a Welsh rarebit. You only need a couple of teaspoons. A must with the Brie tart on page 149 or serve with the Roquefort Galette (see page 90).

Serves 8

1 large thin-skinned orange, washed and roughly chopped
450g (1 lb) fresh (or frozen and thawed) cranberries
2 tablespoons caster sugar

1 In a food processor, blend the whole washed chopped orange until almost a pulp. Add the cranberries and sugar and continue to blend until the cranberries have been finely chopped.

2 Spoon into a bowl or serving dish, cover and refrigerate until required.

Apple, Raisin and Tomato Relish

This is great with any kind of curry.

Serves 4

> *2 dessert apples, chopped*
> *5 tomatoes, chopped*
> *55g (2 oz) raisins, chopped*
> *½ tablespoon olive oil*
> *juice of 1 lemon*
> *2 tablespoons chopped fresh mint*
> *salt and black pepper*

1 Combine all the ingredients together and season well.

2 Cover and allow to stand for 30 minutes. Spoon into a serving dish and serve.

Banana, Lime and Chilli Relish

Again, great with a curry.

Serves 4

> *2 ripe bananas, peeled and chopped*
> *2 tablespoons unsweetened desiccated coconut*
> *1 fresh green chilli, de-seeded and finely chopped*
> *grated rind and juice of 1 lime*
> *black pepper*

1 Simply combine all the ingredients together.

2 Spoon into a dish and serve.

Onion, Orange and Coriander Relish

Good with anything hot and spicy.

Serves 4

2 large oranges
2 red onions, finely chopped
2 tablespoons chopped fresh coriander
½ tablespoon virgin olive oil
salt and black pepper

1 Using a sharp knife, cut away the peel and pith from the oranges, and roughly chop the flesh.

2 Place the chopped orange with all its juices in a bowl and combine with the remaining ingredients. Season to taste.

3 Allow to stand covered for 30 minutes before serving.

Ginger Relish

Good with cheese, particularly a mild and creamy goat's cheese.
The pear softens the heat and sourness of the ginger.

Serves 4–6

5cm (2 inch) piece of fresh root ginger, peeled and grated
2 tablespoons roughly chopped fresh coriander
juice of ½ orange
1 ripe pear, peeled and roughly chopped
salt and black pepper

1 Place all the ingredients in a small food processor and whizz until well combined.

2 Season well, spoon into a bowl and serve.

Nectarine Relish

Good with cheese or spicy foods. Marries well with Aubergine Steaks (see page 114).

Serves 4–6

3 ripe nectarines, finely diced
1 tablespoon capers, roughly chopped
12 Greek olives, pitted and roughly chopped
1 small red onion, finely chopped
juice and zest of 1 lime
2 tablespoons virgin olive oil
salt and black pepper

1 Simply combine all the ingredients together.
2 Season well and allow to marinate for 30 minutes before serving.

Ⓥ **This would be a great partner to lemon-roasted chicken.**

Apple and Walnut Marmalade

Fabulous with Roquefort cheese and Walnut Bread (see page 96).

Serves 4–6

115g (4 oz) butter
900g (2 lb) dessert apples, washed, cored and quartered
175g (6 oz) soft brown sugar
juice and zest of 1 lemon
2 tablespoons brandy (optional)
225g (8 oz) shelled walnuts, roughly chopped

1 In a large saucepan, melt the butter and add the apples, sugar, lemon juice and zest. Gently stir the ingredients to combine, and cover with a lid. Cook gently, over a low heat, for 15–20 minutes, or until the apples are just soft.
2 Remove the lid and turn the heat to high. Allow the marmalade to cook uncovered, stirring occasionally, for a further 5–6 minutes or until most of the excess liquid has evaporated.
3 Stir in the brandy (if using) and set to one side to cool.
4 When cool, stir in the walnuts and serve.

Plum Marmalade

*Serve hot as a pudding with ice-cream or clotted cream,
or bake it with some Brie.*

Serves 4–6

900g (2 lb) plums, halved and stoned
25g (1 oz) butter
115g (4 oz) soft brown sugar
1 teaspoon ground cinnamon
juice and zest of 1 orange

1 Place all the ingredients in a saucepan and bring to the boil, stirring gently. Cover with a lid and simmer for 5 minutes.
2 Remove the lid and simmer for a further 8–10 minutes or until the plums are just soft. Remove from the heat and serve hot or cold.

Baked Tomato Chutney

*More than just a chutney, this is dead simple and tasty. Use it to top salads,
to go with cheese, and to put on baked potatoes. Its uses are endless,
and it keeps for several days in the refrigerator.*

Serves 4

675g (1½ lb) cherry tomatoes
4 tablespoons olive oil
4 tablespoons balsamic vinegar
3 tablespoons demerara sugar
2 whole dried chillies, crumbled
salt and black pepper

1 Preheat the oven to 220°C/425°F/Gas Mark 7.
2 Place the tomatoes in a shallow ovenproof dish and spoon over the olive oil and vinegar. Scatter over the sugar and chillies, and season well.
3 Bake the tomatoes in the oven for 20–25 minutes or until slightly charred and split, but still whole. Serve warm or cold.

Sesame and Cucumber Pickle

An eastern-style dip which would be good with anything hot and rich (the Crisp Vegetable Black Bean Strudel on page 152, for instance).

Serves 4–6

2 tablespoons sesame seeds
150ml (5 fl oz) rice vinegar
4–5 teaspoons caster sugar
1 fresh red chilli, de-seeded and finely chopped
1 spring onion, finely chopped
¼ cucumber, finely chopped
black pepper

1 Place the sesame seeds in a dry pan over a medium heat. Toast until golden.

2 In a mixing bowl, combine the vinegar, sugar and chilli.

3 Stir in the hot toasted sesame seeds, spring onion and cucumber. Season to taste and add extra sugar if required.

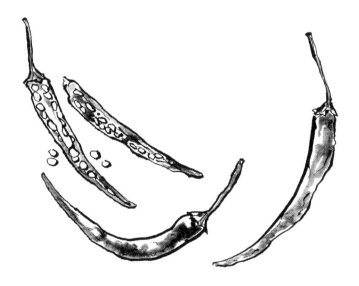

PESTOS AND MAYOS

The pestos here are great for tossing through pasta, spreading on toast, mixing with mashed potatoes and wet polenta, or simply used to top a baked potato. The various mayo ideas are useful in a number of ways, and crop up often throughout the recipes.

Fresh Pesto

Makes about 300ml (10 fl oz)

60g (2¼ oz) basil leaves (that's about 4 packets, or 1 large pot)
55g (2 oz) pine kernels
85–125ml (3–4 fl oz) virgin olive oil to taste
40g (1½ oz) Parmesan cheese, freshly grated
2 garlic cloves, crushed
salt and black pepper

1 Simply place all the ingredients in a food processor, hit the button and whizz until the desired consistency is achieved. The longer you whizz, the smoother the pesto.
2 Put into a bowl or screw-top jar, and store in the refrigerator.

Pea and Ricotta Pesto

Makes about 300ml (10 fl oz)

225g (8 oz) frozen petits pois
3 tablespoons fresh mint leaves
115g (4 oz) ricotta cheese
2 teaspoons lemon juice
salt and black pepper

1 Cook the peas in boiling water until tender. Drain.
2 In a food processor, blend the peas with the remaining ingredients until smoothish. Season well and use immediately.

Broccoli and Cheddar Pesto

Makes a very thick 300ml (10 fl oz)

350g (12 oz) broccoli florets
1 garlic clove
25g (1 oz) mature Cheddar cheese, grated
50ml (2 fl oz) olive oil
a squeeze of lemon juice
salt and black pepper

1 In a large pan of boiling water, simmer the broccoli with the garlic clove until both are tender. Drain well.

2 Place the garlic and broccoli with the remaining ingredients in a food processor and whizz until smooth. Season to taste.

Avocado Mayo

Serves 4–6

2 medium, ripe avocados, stoned and peeled
1 small onion, grated
lime juice to taste
1 tablespoon tomato chutney
1 tablespoon virgin olive oil
1 ripe tomato, finely chopped
1 garlic clove, crushed
1–2 fresh green chillies, de-seeded and finely chopped
salt and black pepper

1 In a bowl, mash the avocado.

2 Stir in the remaining ingredients. Season to taste and serve at once.

Classic Mayo

Serves 3–4

1 egg yolk
a pinch of salt
150ml (5 fl oz) virgin olive oil (or a mixture of virgin and sunflower oils)
black pepper
a squeeze of lemon juice

1 Place the egg yolk and salt in a small bowl or jug and lightly whisk together.

2 Very gradually, drip by drip, begin to add the oil, whilst whisking continuously. Continue in this way until about half the oil has been incorporated. The remaining oil can be added slightly faster, whilst still whisking continuously.

3 Season with black pepper and a squeeze of lemon juice.

Garlic Mayo

Stir in 2 crushed garlic cloves with the black pepper and lemon juice.

Basil Mayo

In a blender or small food processor, whizz together 4 tablespoons mayonnaise, 1 large bunch of fresh basil and 2 tablespoons water.

MARINADES

Amarinade can be spicy, herby or acidic, dry, wet or paste-like. Their purpose is to add flavour, to tenderise and to aid in cooking.

Tarragon Herb Paste

Good tossed through about 450g (1 lb) mushrooms (see page 129), or it can serve as a sauce with grilled vegetables or chips.

Makes about 150ml (5 fl oz)

2 tablespoons fresh tarragon leaves
4 tablespoons fresh flat-leaf parsley
2 garlic cloves
½ tablespoon Dijon mustard
85ml (3 fl oz) olive oil
juice of 1 lemon
salt and black pepper

1 Place all the ingredients in a food processor and whizz until green and creamy.
2 Season well, and use.

Dry Spice

These spices are great tossed through diced aubergine, potatoes or parsnips before baking or roasting (see page 105).

2 teaspoons cumin seeds
6 cardamom pods
2 teaspoons coriander seeds
1 bay leaf
1 dried chilli
1 teaspoon salt
2 tablespoons sunflower oil
black pepper

1 Using a pestle and mortar, blend together the cumin, cardamom, coriander, bay leaf, dried chilli and salt. Mix in the oil and season with black pepper.
2 Use for coating vegetables (it will do about 450g/1 lb).

Orange and Shallot Marinade

This is great for root vegetables, marrow, pumpkin and squashes (see page 109).

3 large shallots, cut into chunks
juice and zest of 2 large oranges
4 tablespoons olive oil
½ teaspoon freshly grated nutmeg
salt and black pepper

1 Combine all the ingredients together.
2 Use to marinate your favourite vegetables before grilling or roasting (it will flavour about 900g/2 lb of vegetables).

STOCKS

Stocks can be frozen or stored in the refrigerator for several days. They can be used as bases for soups and sauces.

Many of you might not want to make your own stock, and would use a vegetable stock cube instead, but by making a stock at home, not only do you know exactly what has gone into it, but the flavour is far better – and the fragrance throughout the house is much more effective than any air-freshener!

Oriental Stock

This is a clean-tasting and aromatic stock which would be best used in spicy dishes, or is good with some noodles dropped in, seasoned and then garnished with some sesame oil and fresh coriander.

Makes about 1.2 litres (2 pints) stock

2.4 litres (4 pints) water

7.5cm (3 inch) piece of fresh root ginger, peeled and cut into thin slices

1 lemongrass stalk, peeled

3 kaffir lime leaves, broken up

2 teaspoons coriander seeds

3 dried chillies

3 whole garlic cloves, unpeeled

2 star anise

1 Place all the ingredients in a saucepan, bring to the boil and simmer gently for 1 hour.

2 Allow to cool, then refrigerate. Strain when needed.

Root Vegetable Stock

*This is quite a sweet vegetable stock, with a gentle kick from the rosemary.
Good for soups or stews or as a broth simply thickened with pearl barley
or lentils and well seasoned to taste.*

Makes about 1.2 litres (2 pints) stock

2.4 litres (4 pints) water

1 leek, cut into thick strips

1 large carrot, peeled and cut into thick strips

2 parsnips, peeled and cut into thick strips

2 small turnips, peeled and cut into strips

1 large sprig of rosemary

1 Place all the ingredients in a large saucepan, bring to the boil and simmer gently for 1 hour.

2 Allow to cool, then strain and refrigerate. Use as required.

Bouquet Garni Stock

This is a mainstay stock, a good base for most purposes.

Makes about 1.2 litres (2 pints) stock

2.4 litres (4 pints) water

2 bay leaves

2 celery sticks, roughly chopped

16 black peppercorns

2 large fresh thyme sprigs

a handful of parsley stalks

1 onion, cut into wedges

1 Place all the ingredients in a large saucepan, bring to the boil and simmer gently for 1 hour.

2 Allow to cool, then strain and refrigerate.

Short Orders

Food no longer, thank goodness, is a regimented affair of three items on a plate. Some of my best eats have been dipping in and out of a selection of bowls filled with delicious morsels.

These short orders are of course great as a nibble with drinks, but they would sit equally well as light dishes for brunch or lunch. They make excellent dinner-party starters, or why not spread out a selection of three or four as an informal buffet-style meal.

These flexible bites are designed to be mixed and matched to your heart's content.

Wrinkled New Potatoes with *Mojos*

This unusual method of cooking potatoes from the Canary Islands makes the skins wrinkly, firm and salty, with a sweet and soft inside. The chilli-based sauce goes well with other grilled vegetables and salads.

Serves 4

450g (1 lb) new potatoes, washed
2 tablespoons salt

For the *mojos:*
2 fresh red chillies, de-seeded and roughly chopped
1 red pepper, de-seeded and roughly chopped
2 garlic cloves, peeled
2 teaspoons ground coriander
1 teaspoon paprika
3 tablespoons olive oil
4 tablespoons white wine vinegar
2 tablespoons water
salt and black pepper

1 Cover the base of a saucepan with the salt. Sit the potatoes on the salt and just cover with water.

2 Bring to the boil and simmer for 10–12 minutes until just cooked. Cover the pan and reduce the heat as low as possible. Simmer for a further 30 minutes.

3 For the *mojos*, simply whizz all the ingredients together in a food processor or liquidiser until just smooth.

4 Serve each portion of wrinkled potatoes with some *mojos* sauce.

Ⓥ **The potatoes and their sauce are both great served as an accompaniment to char-grilled chicken or fish.**

Gingered Green Beans

*The ginger, orange and turmeric add a fresh, zingy flavour
to these traditional green beans.*

Serves 4

450g (1 lb) dwarf beans, topped
1 tablespoon sunflower oil
5cm (2 inch) piece of fresh root ginger, peeled and finely chopped
1 garlic clove, crushed
1 teaspoon ground turmeric
3 tablespoons light soy sauce
juice of 1 large orange
1 teaspoon sesame oil
2 tablespoons warm toasted sesame seeds
black pepper

1 Place the beans in a saucepan of boiling water and cook until just tender.

2 Meanwhile, heat the sunflower oil in a small saucepan and gently fry the ginger and garlic for 30 seconds. Add the turmeric and remove from the heat. Stir in the soy sauce, orange juice and sesame oil.

3 Drain the beans well and return to the saucepan. Pour over the ginger and orange dressing and toss together.

4 Transfer the beans with their dressing to a serving dish, and sprinkle with the warm toasted sesame seeds. Serve hot or at room temperature.

Skillet Asparagus

*Serve with the Baked Lemon and Thyme Risotto (see page 62),
with shavings of Parmesan cheese and warm bread, or the spears
are delicious rolled up in an omelette.*

Serves 4

1 tablespoon olive oil
25g (1 oz) butter
225g (8 oz) asparagus spears, trimmed and halved if very thick
salt and black pepper

1 In a large shallow pan, heat the oil and butter. Put in the asparagus and gently fry for 2 minutes.

2 Cover the pan with a lid and cook for a further 4–7 minutes, until the asparagus is just cooked. Season well.

> ⓥ This asparagus can be used as an accompaniment to grilled chicken or salmon.

Butter-baked Tomatoes

A simple but striking way of serving your tomatoes. Truly mouth-watering, especially with the Garlic Doorsteps on page 98.

Serves 4

8 medium, very ripe tomatoes
1 teaspoon sugar
salt and black pepper
55g (2 oz) unsalted butter
1 fresh red chilli, de-seeded and finely chopped
1 fresh green chilli, de-seeded and finely chopped
1 garlic clove, crushed
140g (5 oz) black Greek olives, pitted and roughly chopped

1 Preheat the oven to 200°C/400°F/Gas Mark 6.

2 With a small, sharp knife, cut a deep cross on the bottom of each tomato (the end opposite the stalk). Using the palm of your hand push down on the cut cross to flatten the tomatoes slightly.

3 Place the tomatoes, cut side up, in a shallow, ovenproof serving dish or plate and sprinkle with the sugar. Season well and set to one side.

4 In a small saucepan gently melt the butter, and stir in the chilli and garlic. Remove from the heat.

5 Spoon the olives into the tomatoes and pour over the chilli butter. Bake the tomatoes for 10–12 minutes or until sizzling hot. Serve at once.

Spanish-style Pimentos with Chillies

This dish is fab served with crusty bread to mop up the juices, and a large glass of red Rioja.

Serves 4

3 tablespoons olive oil
12 baby red peppers, washed and dried
2 fresh red chillies, washed and dried
2 fresh green chillies, washed and dried
rock salt to serve

1 In a shallow frying pan, heat the olive oil. Add the whole peppers and chillies and fry over a low heat for 2 minutes, until they begin to lightly colour.
2 Cover the pan and reduce the heat. Continue to cook over a very low heat for a further 20–30 minutes until the peppers are just tender. Give the pan an occasional shake to prevent them catching on the base.
3 Serve warm with a mound of salt for dipping and crusty bread for the juices.

Avocado Melt

Warm, grilled avocado and creamy mayo on black bread with crunchy cress makes for a great contrast of textures.

Serves 2

4 thick slices black rye bread
2 tablespoons Garlic Mayo (see page 25)
1 large ripe avocado, stoned, peeled and sliced
1 punnet mustard and cress, snipped
lemon wedges to serve

1 Preheat the grill to its highest setting. Toast the bread quickly.
2 Spread each slice of toast with a little of the garlic mayo. Fan some of the avocado slices on top and drizzle over the remaining mayo.
3 Grill the avocado melts until lightly golden.
4 Place two pieces of toast on each serving plate, scatter with some mustard and cress, and serve with a wedge of lemon.

Hot Olive Pâté

Black and green olives major in this exciting hot pâté. Pile it high on rustic-style garlic bread, or Walnut Bread (see page 96).

Serves 4

2 tablespoons olive oil
1 large onion, finely chopped
1 yellow pepper, de-seeded and diced
1 teaspoon ground cumin
55g (2 oz) green olives, pitted and roughly chopped (leave some whole)
55g (2 oz) black olives, pitted and roughly chopped (leave some whole)
2 tablespoons green olive paste
juice and zest of 1 lemon
2 tablespoons chopped fresh flat-leaf parsley
black pepper

To serve:
about 55g (2 oz) salad leaves
2 Garlic Doorsteps (see page 98), halved

1 Heat the oil in a frying pan and fry the onion for 5 minutes, until softened. Add the yellow pepper and cook for a further 4–5 minutes, until softened.
2 Add the cumin and cook for 1 minute.
3 Stir in the olives, olive paste, lemon juice and zest, and parsley. Season well.
4 To serve, pile some salad leaves on to the garlic doorsteps and top with some hot olive pâté. Serve at once.

Sweet Potato Chips with Lime and Chilli

One of my family favourites. You can cook regular potatoes like this too.

Serves 4

675g (1½ lb) sweet potato, scrubbed and cut into large chips
2 tablespoons olive oil
2 tablespoons soy sauce
black pepper
freshly grated nutmeg (optional)

For the butter:

85g (3 oz) unsalted butter

2 fresh red chillies, de-seeded and finely chopped

juice and zest of 1 lime

1 Preheat the oven to 200°C/400°F/Gas Mark 6.
2 In a large bowl, toss the sweet potato chips with the olive oil and soy sauce. Transfer to a large roasting tin and season with black pepper and nutmeg.
3 Bake in the preheated oven for 30–40 minutes until golden and crisp.
4 Meanwhile, place the butter, chilli and lime juice and zest in a small saucepan. Place over a low heat and heat very gently to melt the butter and combine with the other ingredients.
5 Serve the sweet potato chips hot, to dip into the lime and chilli butter on the side.

Mozzarella Ravigote

A simple mouth-watering starter. The piquant ravigote salsa works well with the creamy thick mozzarella cheese, or is great served on grilled vegetables.

Serves 4

2 tablespoons Greek black olives, pitted and roughly chopped

2 tablespoons baby caper berries

1 plum tomato, roughly chopped

1 shallot, very finely chopped

3 tablespoons virgin olive oil

1 tablespoon fresh thyme leaves

juice of ½ lemon

a pinch of sugar

black pepper

225g (8 oz) mozzarella cheese, sliced into rounds

1 In a bowl combine the olives, capers, tomato, shallot, olive oil and thyme. Season with the lemon juice, sugar and black pepper and set to one side.
2 Arrange the mozzarella on one large plate, or four individual plates.
3 Spoon the olive dressing over the mozzarella slices and serve with warm crusty bread.

> ⓥ **Serve the ravigote salsa as an accompaniment to a selection of cured meats in place of the mozzarella.**

Sliced Goat's Cheese with Beetroot Caviar

The tart richness of the goat's cheese works a treat
with the faintly sweet beetroot.

Serves 4

2 × 140g (5 oz) mild soft goat's cheeses
1 small head fennel, finely chopped (reserve the fennel tops for decoration)
2 shallots, finely chopped
grated zest of 1 lemon
2 tablespoons lemon juice
2 tablespoons virgin olive oil
salt and black pepper
115g (4 oz) cooked beetroot, peeled and finely chopped

1 Chill the goat's cheeses well, which will make slicing easier.
2 In a mixing bowl, combine the fennel, shallot, lemon zest and juice and the olive oil. Season well. Cover and set to one side for 2 hours to allow the flavours to develop.
3 Using a sharp knife, slice the mounds of goat's cheese horizontally into 4 rough slices (don't worry if they squash slightly, it doesn't matter). Carefully place the slices of cheese, slightly overlapping, on a large, shallow serving dish or plate. Grind over some black pepper.
4 Just before serving, gently stir the chopped beetroot into the fennel mixture. Spoon this mixture over the goat's cheese slices, and decorate with the reserved feathery fennel tops.

Baked Goat's Cheese with Pomegranate Relish

The tang of the pomegranate relish is absolutely scrummy with the baked goat's cheese.

Serves 2

1 large thick slice of rustic bread, cut in half
125g (4½ oz) Camembert-style goat's cheese
1 orange, peeled and segmented
1 pomegranate, halved and seeds scooped out
black pepper

1 Preheat the oven to 200°C/400°F/Gas Mark 6.

2 Lightly toast the pieces of bread.

3 Slice the goat's cheese in half horizontally and place each half on top of a toasted bread *croûte*. Bake in the preheated oven for 4–5 minutes or until the cheese is just melted.

4 Meanwhile, simply combine the orange segments with the pomegranate seeds, and season with lots of black pepper.

5 Place each *croûte* on a large dinner plate and top with a spoonful of relish. Serve at once.

Pan-fried Halloumi Cheese

Serve the fried cheese with the sweetcorn and pineapple salsa on page 14 – they're fantastic together.

Serves 4 as a starter

250g (9 oz) halloumi cheese, drained and rinsed
plain flour, seasoned
2 tablespoons olive oil
½ teaspoon hot paprika
1 tablespoon fresh flat-leaf parsley leaves

To serve:
Pineapple and Roasted Sweetcorn Salsa (see page 14)

1 Dry the halloumi cheese well on kitchen paper and cut into slices about 1cm (½ inch) wide. Dip the cheese slices in the seasoned flour.

2 In a frying pan, heat the olive oil, then add the coated cheese slices and fry for 1–2 minutes each side until golden brown. When cooked on both sides, sprinkle the paprika and parsley leaves over the pan contents.

3 Remove the pan from the heat, and serve the cheese slices on individual serving plates with the salsa.

Indian Baked Nuts

These spicy gems are very more-ish.

Serves 6–8

2 tablespoons grapeseed or sunflower oil
1 teaspoon ground cumin
1 teaspoon ground coriander
2 teaspoons hot paprika
salt and black pepper
115g (4 oz) whole almonds
115g (4 oz) pecan nuts
115g (4 oz) cashew nuts
115g (4 oz) Brazil nuts

1 Preheat the oven to 200°C/400°F/Gas Mark 6.

2 In a large bowl combine the oil with the spices, including salt and pepper. Add the nuts and toss together well.

3 Transfer the coated nuts to a baking sheet and bake for 8–10 minutes until lightly toasted. Serve warm.

Salad SENSATIONS

S alads are probably some of the most valuable dishes you can
have at your fingertips. From breakfast and brunch through
to supper and pudding, the possibilities are endless.
Remember a salad doesn't necessarily need leaves, or for that matter
to be served in the summer. The Warm Winter Salad or the Oriental
Chip Salad, for instance, will certainly heat you through on the
coldest winter day.

   And salads aren't always lightweight. Try the Thai salad with
oodles of noodles for a substantial supper dish. Fresh, colourful, crisp,
interesting, hot, warm, cold, seasonal and simple to prepare, this
chapter is dedicated to the super salad, completely 'dressed to thrill'.

Grilled Fennel Steaks with Roquefort Dressing

This is a lovely and simple way of preparing and cooking fennel.
If you can, use continental-style salad leaves.

Serves 4 as a starter, 2 as a main course

2 bulbs of fennel, trimmed and thickly sliced
olive oil
salt and black pepper
85g (3 oz) salad leaves to serve

For the dressing:
115g (4 oz) Roquefort cheese, crumbled
3 tablespoons fromage frais
4–5 tablespoons fresh orange juice
½ bunch of fresh chives, chopped

1 Place the fennel in a steamer and steam for 10 minutes or until just tender. Dry well on kitchen paper.

2 Preheat the grill to a medium setting.

3 Brush the fennel generously with olive oil and season well. Place under the grill and grill for 8–10 minutes on each side until brown.

4 Meanwhile, in a bowl, combine all the dressing ingredients together until almost smooth and season with black pepper.

5 To serve, arrange the crisp salad leaves on individual plates, and place the fennel steaks on top. Hand the Roquefort dressing separately.

> ⊗ **Serve fillet steak with the sauce in place of the fennel.**

Thai Paw

*Tantalising for the taste buds, this is clean and light, and refreshingly good!
Try it after an exceedingly hot curry, or as a starter to a spicy meal.*

Serves 2

juice of 1 lime
1 fresh red chilli, de-seeded and finely chopped
2 spring onions, sliced on a slant
1 large, just ripe paw-paw (or mango)
salt and black pepper
1 bunch of fresh coriander
lime wedges to serve

1 In a small bowl, combine the lime juice, chilli and spring onion.

2 Quarter the paw-paw and scoop out the seeds. Using a small sharp knife, remove the skin and cut the flesh into large, bite-sized chunks.

3 Add the paw-paw to the chilli and onion mixture and season well. Gently stir in the coriander leaves.

4 To serve, pile the Thai Paw in the centre of two serving bowls or plates. Add the lime wedges for an extra kick.

Sautéed Radishes with Black Pepper Cheese

An unusual and delicious way of serving radishes.

Serves 4

40g (1½ oz) unsalted butter
2 bunches of radishes, trimmed but green stem still intact
1 teaspoon runny honey
200g (7 oz) cream cheese
black pepper
warm crusty bread

1 In a large frying pan, heat the butter. Add the radishes and honey and stir-fry for 1 minute.

2 Season the cream cheese, heavily, with freshly ground black pepper. Mix in well.

3 Divide the hot radishes between four serving plates. Spoon the peppered cheese to one side, and serve with a thick slice of warm bread.

Chilli Grape Salad with Watercress

This snazzy, Spanish-style salad is wonderful served on creamy ricotta cheese. Serve with warm buttered toast or crusty bread.

Serves 4

250g (9 oz) ricotta cheese
85g (3 oz) watercress

For the chilli grape salad:
6 ripe plum tomatoes, diced
175g (6 oz) seedless red grapes, halved
¼ cucumber, finely chopped
1 red pepper, de-seeded and finely chopped
2 tablespoons roughly chopped fresh basil leaves
juice of 1 lemon
1 tablespoon virgin olive oil
2 teaspoons chilli sauce, or to taste
salt and black pepper

1 In a bowl, combine all the chilli grape salad ingredients together. Season well and set to one side.

2 Spread the ricotta cheese over the base of a large serving plate. Surround the ricotta with a ring of watercress and top the ricotta with the chilli grape salad.

Carrot Soup and Salad

A sumptuous way of combining soup and, yes, salad!

Serves 4

1 tablespoon olive oil
1 small onion, chopped
675g (1½ lb) carrots, peeled and sliced
1.2 litres (2 pints) Bouquet Garni Stock (see page 29), or stock made from a cube
salt and black pepper
2 tablespoons Greek-style yoghurt

For the salad:
4 carrots, cut into ribbons
1 small red onion, finely sliced
2 tablespoons fresh basil leaves
2 teaspoons virgin olive oil
2 oranges, segmented, juice reserved

1 In a large saucepan, heat the oil, add the onion and fry for 5 minutes or until slightly softened. Add the carrots and cook for a further 2 minutes.
2 Add the vegetable stock and season with salt and pepper to taste. Bring to the boil and simmer for 20–25 minutes or until the carrots are soft.
3 Meanwhile, place all the salad ingredients in a bowl, toss together and season with salt and pepper. Set to one side.
4 Place the soup in a blender and whizz until smooth, adding some water if it is too thick.
5 To serve, pour the soup into four shallow soup dishes. Drizzle the top of each with some yoghurt and pile a mound of carrot salad in the centre. Serve at once.

Warm Winter Salad

This is a luscious way of spicing up your roots!

Serves 4

5 medium parsnips, peeled and halved lengthwise
5 medium carrots, peeled and halved lengthwise
1 large red onion, cut into wedges
5 small turnips, peeled and halved
225g (8 oz) baby new potatoes, halved if too large
6 garlic cloves, unpeeled
4 tablespoons olive oil
150ml (5 fl oz) white wine
salt and black pepper
225g (8 oz) Brussels sprouts, trimmed

For the dressing:
2 tablespoons grainy mustard
1 tablespoon walnut oil
1 tablespoon white wine vinegar
5 tablespoons olive oil

1 Preheat the oven to 200°C/400°F/Gas Mark 6.
2 Place the parsnip, carrot, red onion, turnip, new potatoes and whole garlic cloves in a large roasting tin. Spoon over the olive oil and wine and season well.
3 Cover and bake in the preheated oven for 20 minutes, then remove the cover and bake for a further 40 minutes or until the vegetables are just tender and crisped.
4 Meanwhile, in a large pan of boiling water, simmer the sprouts until just tender.
5 In a small bowl, combine all the dressing ingredients together and season.
6 To serve, toss the warm roasted vegetables with the sprouts and turn into a large serving dish. Pour over the dressing and serve at once.

King Cos Salad with Spiced *Croûtes* and Creamy Avocado Dressing

To my mind, the cos lettuce is completely underrated. Use it as the crisp, crunchy foundation to this warm salad.

Serves 4

3 oranges
1 large ripe avocado, halved, stoned and peeled
2 tablespoons water
juice of ½ lemon
salt and black pepper
1 cos lettuce, washed and torn into large pieces

For the *croûtes*:
2 tablespoons olive oil
1 teaspoon ground cumin
1 teaspoon ground coriander
3 thick slices rustic-style bread, cut into bite-sized pieces

1 Preheat the oven to 220°C/425°F/Gas Mark 7.

2 In a bowl mix together the olive oil and the spices. Add the bread *croûtes* and toss together. Place the *croûtes* on a baking sheet and bake in the preheated oven for 5 minutes or so, until golden.

3 Using a small, sharp knife, remove the peel and pith from the oranges, and segment them, reserving any juices.

4 In a food processor, blend half the avocado flesh with the water, lemon juice and reserved orange juice. Season well.

5 Divide the cos lettuce between four large dinner plates and drizzle over the avocado dressing. Scatter over the orange segments and remaining avocado, cut into slices.

6 Place the hot *croûtes* over and around the salad and finish with a grinding of black pepper. Serve at once.

> ⊗ **The orange segments can be replaced with 4 rashers streaky bacon, grilled until crisp, and chopped.**

Oriental Chip Salad with Cashew Sauce

Based on a salad I had in Thailand. Try this unusual way of serving chips, topped with a scrummy, warm cashew sauce.

Serves 4

For the chips:
900g (2 lb) potatoes
3 tablespoons olive oil
3 tablespoons dark soy sauce
black pepper

For the sauce:
150ml (5 fl oz) sunflower oil
200g (7 oz) cashew nuts
2 garlic cloves, chopped
2 tablespoons dark soy sauce
juice of 2 limes
250ml (9 fl oz) water
2 tablespoons roughly chopped
   fresh coriander

For the salad:
140g (5 oz) beansprouts
115g (4 oz) watercress
2 carrots, cut into ribbons
2 teaspoons sunflower oil
1 teaspoon rice vinegar

To serve:
2 limes, halved

1 Preheat the oven to 200°C/400°F/Gas Mark 6.

2 Cut the potatoes into very thick chips and place in a large, non-stick roasting pan. Pour over the oil and soy sauce and toss together. Season with black pepper.

3 Bake in the preheated oven for 35–40 minutes, turning occasionally, until golden brown and crisp.

4 For the sauce, in a frying pan, heat the sunflower oil and fry the cashew nuts until golden. Add the garlic, soy sauce and lime juice (the pan will hiss dramatically). Remove from the heat and stir in the water and coriander. Set to one side for 2 minutes.

5 Place the beansprouts, watercress, and carrot ribbons in a bowl. Combine the sunflower oil with the rice vinegar and use to dress the salad ingredients, then arrange on a large serving plate.

6 Transfer the cashew sauce to a liquidiser and whizz until smooth.

7 To serve, pile the salad onto a large plate, top with a pile of the cooked chips and spoon over some of the warm cashew sauce. Squeeze over some lime juice for extra zing. Hand the remaining sauce separately and serve at once.

Tarragon Eggs with Mixed Leaves

A lightly cooked omelette, served on salad leaves, topped with a tarragon dressing.

Serves 2

4 eggs
1 spring onion, finely sliced
salt and black pepper
25g (1 oz) butter

For the dressing:
1 bunch of fresh tarragon
juice of ½ lemon
3 tablespoons olive oil

To serve:
60–85g (2–3 oz) salad leaves
175g (6 oz) cherry tomatoes, halved

1 Pick the leaves from the tarragon stems and place them in a blender or small food processor. Add the lemon juice and olive oil and whizz together. Season well.

2 Crack the eggs into a small bowl and whisk to break up. Stir in the spring onion and season with salt and pepper.

3 Heat the butter in a large frying pan, until foaming. Add the omelette mix and cook until golden brown underneath but still slightly soft and runny on the top.

4 Arrange some salad leaves and cherry tomato halves on two large dinner plates. Roughly cut the omelette into large pieces and place on the salad leaves. Spoon over the tarragon dressing and serve at once.

Thai Noodle Salad

This contrast of sweet and spicy flavours has an eastern appeal.
There's no reason why pasta or short-grain brown rice couldn't be used
instead of the noodles for a change.

Serves 4–6

200g (7 oz) thread egg noodles, cooked and drained
115g (4 oz) sugar-snap peas, blanched, refreshed and halved lengthwise
2 large carrots, peeled and cut into very fine strips
175g (6 oz) spring greens, blanched and refreshed
2 tablespoons toasted sesame seeds to garnish

For the dressing:
4 tablespoons sunflower oil
1 bunch of spring onions, cut into chunky strips
3 tablespoons light soy sauce
juice of 1 large orange
5cm (2 inch) piece of fresh root ginger, peeled and grated
1 large garlic clove, crushed
1 teaspoon chopped lemongrass (optional)
2 teaspoons sesame oil
black pepper

1   In a frying pan, heat 1 tablespoon of the sunflower oil and stir-fry the spring onion for 30 seconds. Remove from the heat and stir in the remaining dressing ingredients. Season to taste.

2   In a mixing bowl, combine all the salad ingredients and toss with the warm dressing.

3   Mound portions of the noodle salad on to large dinner plates, scatter each with some toasted sesame seeds and serve at once.

> ⓥ **The sugar-snap peas and sesame seeds can be replaced by 140g (5 oz) white crab meat.**

Stunning Staples

When most people think of staples in the diet, bread, potatoes, pasta and rice are the first things that come to mind. But in fact the choice of staples now available is broader than it has ever been!

Try couscous with roasted vegetables and tahini cream or onion steaks on bulgar wheat with basil butter and butternut squash, and you will see that staples are great carriers of flavour. In the same way that an envelope carries a letter, the two work best when used together.

Of course the traditional staples have not been neglected, just given a new twist. My favourite hangover cure, for instance, is chillied eggs on onion rice! For the humble British potato, Roquefort cabbage gives good old bubble and squeak a fabulous make-over. And also included are some new recipes for the versatile sweet potato.

Cracked Wheat Pilaff with Spiced Fruits

Bulgar wheat, sometimes known as cracked wheat, is a staple in Middle Eastern countries. It is one of my favourite cereals, nutty, light and moist, and is excellent served in place of rice, pasta or potatoes or used in stuffings.

Serves 4

225g (8 oz) bulgar wheat, rinsed
1 tablespoon sunflower oil
1 large onion, chopped
1 garlic clove, crushed
2 teaspoons ground turmeric
2 teaspoons ground cumin
1 teaspoon ground coriander
1 cinnamon stick, split
115g (4 oz) dried apricots, chopped
115g (4 oz) raisins
1 bay leaf
2 large carrots, peeled and grated
600–850ml (1–1½ pints) Root Vegetable Stock (see page 29), or stock made from a cube
salt and black pepper
55g (2 oz) flaked almonds, toasted
2 tablespoons roughly chopped fresh coriander
1 large lemon, cut into wedges

1 In a bowl, soak the bulgar wheat in enough water to cover, for 15 minutes.

2 Meanwhile, heat the oil in a large frying pan or wok and cook the onion for 5 minutes, until softened. Add the garlic, turmeric, cumin, coriander and cinnamon to the pan, and cook for a further minute.

3 Add the fruits, bay leaf and carrot to the onion, and pour in 600ml (1 pint) of the stock. Drain the bulgar wheat and add to the pan. Season well.

4 Cover and cook the pilaff for a further 10–15 minutes, adding extra stock if the pan becomes too dry. The pilaff should be risotto-like.

5 Spoon the pilaff into a large serving dish and stir in the nuts and coriander, reserving a tablespoon of each to scatter over the top. Surround the pilaff with the lemon wedges and serve at once.

Mediterranean Vegetable Couscous with Tahini Cream

The tahini adds a delicious, creamy richness to the couscous and vegetables.

Serves 4

1 red pepper, de-seeded
1 yellow pepper, de-seeded
1 large aubergine
2 medium courgettes
1 large red onion
3 tablespoons olive oil
salt and black pepper
250g (9 oz) cherry tomatoes

For the couscous:
250g (9 oz) couscous
2 tablespoons olive oil
juice of ½ lemon

For the tahini cream:
3 tablespoons tahini paste
juice of 1 small orange
85g (3 oz) Greek-style yoghurt
1 teaspoon ground cumin
paprika for dusting
2 tablespoons roughly chopped fresh
   flat-leaf parsley

1 Preheat the oven to 220°C/425°F/Gas Mark 7.

2 Prepare the peppers, aubergine and courgettes by cutting into chunks of about 4cm (1½ inches). Cut the onion into wedges. Place the prepared vegetables in a roasting tin and toss with the olive oil. Season well.

3 Roast in the preheated oven for 20 minutes, then add the cherry tomatoes and roast for a further 20 minutes until cooked and lightly charred.

4 For the tahini cream, in a bowl combine the tahini paste with the orange juice. Add the yoghurt and cumin and season to taste. Set to one side.

5 Cook the couscous as directed on the packet. When cooked toss the warm couscous in the olive oil and lemon juice, and season well.

6 To serve, spread the couscous out on a large serving dish. Pile the roasted vegetables on top. Serve the tahini cream on the side in a separate serving bowl, and sprinkle the surface with a little paprika and the freshly chopped parsley. This dish is delicious warm or cold.

> Ⓥ **Serve the vegetable couscous with roast leg of lamb instead of the normal accompaniments.**

Onion Steaks
with Warm Sesame Couscous

Perhaps you've never thought of using onions as the centre of a dish, but these caramelised, mustard onions work a treat and look stunning.

Serves 4

4 medium red onions, cut horizontally into slices 1cm (½ inch) thick
4 tablespoons olive oil
2 tablespoons grainy mustard
2 tablespoons water
¼ teaspoon sugar
salt and black pepper

For the couscous:
450g (1 lb) couscous
115g (4 oz) sesame seeds, toasted
1 bunch of fresh mint, roughly chopped

To serve:
115g (4 oz) baby spinach leaves
juice of ½ lemon

1 Put the onion steaks in a dish in one layer. In a bowl, combine all the remaining onion ingredients together and season well. Pour over the onion and set to one side for 30 minutes.
2 Preheat the oven to 220°C/425°F/Gas Mark 7.
3 Place the onion steaks on a baking sheet with their marinade. Roast in the preheated oven for 40–45 minutes, until lightly browned in places.
4 Cook the couscous as directed on the packet. Stir in the sesame seeds and mint. Season well.
5 To serve, toss the baby spinach leaves in the lemon juice and season. Divide between four serving plates and top with the onion steaks and their marinade juices. Serve the couscous in a bowl and hand separately.

Basil Butter Bulgar with Butternut Squash

The basil and lemon add a fresh flavour to this nutty and buttery bulgar dish.

Serves 4

450g (1 lb) red onions, cut into thick wedges
675g (1½ lb) butternut squash, peeled, de-seeded and cut into 4–5cm (2 inch) pieces
2 tablespoons olive oil
salt and black pepper
225g (8 oz) bulgar wheat, rinsed
85g (3 oz) unsalted butter
juice of ½ lemon
1 bunch of fresh basil leaves

1 Preheat the oven to 200°C/400°F/Gas Mark 6.

2 In a large roasting tin, combine the red onion with the butternut squash and olive oil. Season well. Bake in the preheated oven for 55–60 minutes, until the vegetables are cooked and slightly charred.

3 Meanwhile, place the bulgar wheat in a large bowl and cover with boiling water. Set to one side for 30 minutes, then drain.

4 In a large frying pan heat the butter. Add the lemon juice and basil leaves to the pan: everything will become bright green. Immediately add the drained bulgar and toss in the dressing for 2–3 minutes or until warmed through. Season well.

5 To serve, spread the basil bulgar on a large flat serving dish. Pile the roasted vegetables on top and serve at once.

Herb Polenta Slabs

These cheesy and herby polenta slabs are wonderful served with any salad, but are particularly good with the Red Fire Ragoût (see page 117) or the Aubergine and Apple Ragoût (see page 104).

Serves 4

850ml (1½ pints) Bouquet Garni or Root Vegetable Stock (see page 29), or stock made with a cube
150ml (5 fl oz) white wine
225g (8 oz) quick-cook instant polenta
2 tablespoons roughly chopped fresh basil
3 tablespoons roughly chopped fresh chives
85g (3 oz) Parmesan cheese, grated
salt and black pepper

1 In a large saucepan heat the stock and wine together. Bring to the boil and simmer for 5 minutes. Gradually add the polenta to the pan, stirring continually. Simmer for 1 minute, stirring all the time.

2 Remove the polenta from the heat and stir in the herbs and half of the grated Parmesan. Season well.

3 Pour the polenta into a shallow tin or tray about 35 × 23cm (14 × 9 inches). Set to one side for an hour.

4 When the polenta is set, cut out eight slabs and place on a baking sheet. Preheat the grill.

5 Sprinkle the polenta slabs with the remaining Parmesan and place under the grill until the polenta is golden brown and hot.

Barley Risotto

The much underrated pearl barley is the main ingredient in this dish, along with Roquefort cheese and toasted hazelnuts. A really gutsy risotto, which is delicious served with a watercress salad.

Serves 4

225g (8 oz) pearl barley
1 tablespoon olive oil
1 onion, chopped
1 red pepper, de-seeded and diced
600–850ml (1–1½ pints) Root Vegetable Stock (see page 29),
　　or stock made from a cube
salt and black pepper
115g (4 oz) frozen petits pois
115g (4 oz) Roquefort cheese, crumbled
100g (3½ oz) warm roasted hazelnuts
1 bunch of fresh flat-leaf parsley

1 Wash the barley and soak in cold water to cover for 30 minutes.

2 In a large saucepan, heat the oil and gently fry the onion and diced pepper for 5 minutes, until softened. Add the drained barley and 750ml (1¼ pints) of the stock and season well.

3 Bring to the boil and simmer gently for 30–35 minutes until the barley is just tender, adding more liquid to the pan if necessary. About 5 minutes before the end of the cooking time, add the peas and simmer for the remaining 5 minutes.

4 Stir the Roquefort cheese, hazelnuts and parsley through the risotto and serve at once.

Baked Lemon and Thyme Risotto

An easy, non-stir risotto that's baked in the oven. Serve it with Skillet Asparagus (see page 32), or Butter-baked Tomatoes (see page 33).

Serves 4

1 large onion, chopped
55g (2 oz) butter
350g (12 oz) risotto rice
about 1.2 litres (2 pints) Bouquet Garni or Root Vegetable Stock (see page 29),
*   or stock made with a cube*
juice and zest of 2 lemons
1 bunch of fresh thyme, roughly chopped
85g (3 oz) Parmesan cheese, grated
salt and black pepper

1 Preheat the oven to 200°C/400°F/Gas Mark 6.

2 In a large frying pan, gently fry the onion in the butter for 5 minutes, until softened. Stir in the rice then pour in two-thirds of the stock.

3 Bring to the boil and transfer to a large shallow ovenproof dish. Cover the dish and place in the preheated oven for 20 minutes.

4 Remove the risotto from the oven and turn the oven up to 220°C/425°F/Gas Mark 7.

5 Add the remaining stock, the lemon juice and zest, thyme and Parmesan to the risotto, and season well. Return to the oven, uncovered, to cook for a further 10–12 minutes or until the rice is just cooked. The risotto should still be moist, but slightly crisp on top.

Fragrant Orange Rice

Using a whole orange in this dish gives maximum flavour. Choose a thin-skinned orange for the best result. The rice goes well with most of the lentil dishes – and my favourite is the Garlic Dhal with Date and Coriander Raita (see pages 83 and 12).

Serves 4

350g (12 oz) basmati rice, washed well
1 tablespoon sunflower oil
1 large onion, chopped
4 bay leaves
5cm (2 inch) piece of cinnamon stick, split
4 star anise
2 tablespoons desiccated coconut
1 small orange, washed and blended or chopped to a pulp
juice and grated zest of 2 lemons
600ml (1 pint) water
salt and black pepper

1 Soak the rice in cold water for 20 minutes, then drain well.

2 In a saucepan, heat the oil and fry the onion for 5–6 minutes until golden brown. Add the bay leaves, cinnamon, star anise and coconut and gently cook for a further minute.

3 Add the chopped orange, lemon juice and zest. Stir in the drained rice and cook for a further 3 minutes. Pour in the water and season well. Bring the contents of the pan to the boil and simmer for 10–12 minutes or until the liquid has been absorbed and the rice is just tender.

4 Turn off the heat and cover the saucepan with a lid. Allow the rice to stand for 2–3 minutes. Just before serving, separate and fluff up the rice with a fork.

> ⊗ **This rice is excellent served with a creamy korma-style curry.**

Chillied Eggs on Onion Rice

A healthier style of fried eggs with an oriental twist,
which makes for a great hangover cure.

Serves 2

175g (6 oz) basmati rice
300ml (10 fl oz) tomato passata
2–3 teaspoons hot chilli sauce
1 teaspoon sugar
salt and black pepper
2 tablespoons grapeseed oil
1 bunch of spring onions, roughly chopped
2 large eggs
2 tablespoons fresh coriander leaves
½ fresh red chilli, de-seeded and cut into slivers

1 Cook the basmati rice as per the instructions on the packet.

2 Meanwhile, in a small saucepan, heat the tomato passata, chilli sauce and sugar. Season to taste and add a little water if necessary to achieve a gravy-like consistency.

3 In a non-stick frying pan, heat 1 tablespoon of the oil and add the spring onion. Fry for 3–4 minutes until golden and soft, then stir into the cooked rice and set to one side.

4 Heat the remaining oil in the frying pan and crack in the eggs. Sprinkle the eggs with the coriander leaves and slivers of chilli. Season well and cover the pan with a lid. Allow the eggs to gently steam until just cooked.

5 To serve, place a dome of onion rice in the centre of two large dinner plates. Place an egg on the top of each dome and drizzle around each dome with some chilli and tomato sauce. Hand the remaining sauce separately.

> ⊗ **Reduce the spring onions to half a bunch, and stir a peppered mackerel fillet, flaked, into the rice with the spring onion at stage 3.**

Oriental Soup

*A creamy coconut oriental feast in a bowl. Spaghetti or egg noodles
can be used in place of the rice.*

Serves 4

½ tablespoon sunflower oil
1 bunch of spring onions, roughly chopped
2 teaspoons chopped fresh lemongrass
2 kaffir lime leaves, crumbled
5cm (2 inch) piece of fresh root ginger, peeled and grated
1 garlic clove, crushed
1 × 400ml (14 fl oz) can of coconut milk
600ml (1 pint) Bouquet Garni Stock (see page 29), or stock made with a cube
salt and black pepper
225g (8 oz) petits pois
1 large fresh red chilli, de-seeded and cut into strips
juice of 1 lime

To serve:
225g (8 oz) cooked basmati or Thai fragrant rice

1 In a saucepan heat the oil. Add the onion, lemongrass, lime leaves, ginger and garlic, and fry for 5 minutes.

2 Add the coconut milk and stock, and season well.

3 Bring to the boil and add the peas and chilli strips. Reduce the heat and simmer for 1–2 minutes until the peas are cooked.

4 Just before serving stir in the lime juice, then place a serving of cooked rice in the centre of each soup bowl and ladle over the oriental soup. Serve at once.

> Ⓥ **175g (6 oz) small raw prawns, peeled, or
> cooked chicken strips can be used to replace the
> peas in stage 3.**

Potato Pie with Rustic Peas

One of my all-time favourites, this is a warming and hearty supper dish.

Serves 4

900g (2 lb) potatoes, peeled and cut into 5cm (2 inch) chunks
1 tablespoon olive oil
2 onions, chopped
2 tablespoons roughly chopped fresh mint leaves
salt and black pepper

For the rustic peas:
1 tablespoon olive oil
1 onion, sliced
2 garlic cloves, crushed
2 large red peppers, de-seeded and thickly sliced
4 small tomatoes, quartered
450g (1 lb) frozen petits pois
150ml (5 fl oz) Bouquet Garni Stock (see page 29), or stock made with a cube
2 large lettuce leaves, shredded

To serve:
150ml (5 fl oz) fromage frais

1 Preheat the oven to 200°C/400°F/Gas Mark 6.
2 Place the potato chunks in a large pan of boiling water. Simmer for 10–12 minutes or until the potatoes are soft.
3 Meanwhile, in a frying pan, heat the oil. Add the onion and gently fry for 10 minutes until softened and browned.
4 Drain the potatoes well, before returning to the pan and mashing. Add the softened onion and the mint and mash to combine. Season well.
5 Spread the mashed potato and onion out on a baking sheet into a circle about 23cm (9 inches) in diameter. Place in the oven and bake for 25–30 minutes until golden.
6 Meanwhile, for the rustic peas, in a saucepan heat the olive oil. Add the onion and fry for 5 minutes until golden. Add the garlic and pepper and fry for a further 5 minutes.
7 Add the tomato and peas. Stir in the stock and season well. Cover and simmer for 2 minutes or until the peas are heated through. Stir in the lettuce.
8 To serve, place wedges of potato on each plate and accompany with a serving of rustic peas, topped with a spoonful of *fromage frais*.

Roquefort Cabbage with Buttermilk Mash

Everyone loves mash, but the buttermilk gives it that extra something. However, Greek-style yoghurt or crème fraîche *work too. And, despite its reputation, red cabbage doesn't have to take hours to cook. Here it is, virtually instant, and in my opinion at its best.*

Serves 4

55g (2 oz) unsalted butter
2 teaspoons walnut oil
1 small red cabbage, quartered, cored and shredded
150ml (5 fl oz) red wine
175g (6 oz) Roquefort cheese, roughly cut into pieces
100g (3½ oz) walnut halves
2 tablespoons fresh thyme leaves
1 fat garlic clove, crushed
salt and black pepper

For the buttermilk mash:
900g (2 lb) potatoes, well scrubbed
300ml (10 fl oz) buttermilk

1 Make the buttermilk mash first. Cut the scrubbed potatoes into small, even-sized pieces (skins left on). Place in a saucepan, cover with water and cook until tender. Drain well, return to the saucepan, and mash with the buttermilk. Season with salt and pepper and keep warm while you cook the cabbage.

2 In a large frying pan or wok heat the butter and oil. Add the cabbage and red wine and cook over a high heat for 4–5 minutes, until the cabbage begins to wilt.

3 Add the cheese, walnuts, thyme and garlic and toss briefly. Season well and serve at once with crusty bread and buttermilk mash.

Chillied Sweet Potatoes with Brown Rice

Sweet potato is a delicious vegetable that always seems to play a supporting role. Here's a dish to give it a lead part. It's served with brown rice which has a delicious nutty flavour.

Serves 4

250g (9 oz) short-grain or easy-cook brown rice
salt and black pepper
1 bunch of fresh coriander, roughly chopped

For the chillied sweet potatoes:
1 tablespoon olive oil
1 large onion, roughly chopped
675g (1½ lb) sweet potatoes, cut into 3–4cm (1–1½ inch) chunks
2 garlic cloves, crushed
1 fresh red chilli, de-seeded and finely chopped
½ teaspoon ground cumin
½ teaspoon ground coriander
½ teaspoon ground turmeric
½ teaspoon paprika
1 × 400ml (14 fl oz) can of coconut milk

1 Cook the brown rice as directed on the packet, seasoning it well.
2 Meanwhile, in a large pan, heat the oil, add the onion and fry for 5 minutes. Add the sweet potato, garlic, chilli and spices and fry for a further 2 minutes.
3 Stir in the coconut milk and season. Cover the pan and simmer for 20–25 minutes, or until the sweet potato is cooked.
4 To serve, pile the cooked brown rice in the centre of four dinner plates, top with some chillied sweet potato and scatter with the coriander. Serve at once.

Baked Sweet Potato with Chilli Cream

A variation on the classic baked potato and soured cream –
the chilli cream works well with the sweetness of the potato.
Baked potatoes will never be the same again!

Serves 4

4 medium sweet potatoes, washed and pricked
1 bunch of fresh coriander
2 limes, halved

For the chilli cream:
300ml (10 fl oz) soured cream or Greek-style yoghurt
zest of 1 lime
1 fresh green chilli, de-seeded and finely chopped
1 fresh red chilli, de-seeded and finely chopped
salt and black pepper

1 Preheat the oven to 200°C/400°F/Gas Mark 6.

2 Bake the sweet potatoes in the preheated oven for about 50–60 minutes or until cooked. Larger potatoes will take a little longer.

3 Meanwhile combine all the cream ingredients together. Season and set to one side.

4 Serve the potatoes, split open and each topped with a dollop of chilli cream. Scatter over the coriander leaves, squeeze over some lime juice, and serve at once.

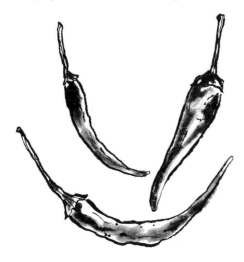

Thai Broth with Crispy Noodles

A stunningly good dish with an array of tastes and textures. I am not one for complicated recipes, but this one is really worth pushing the boat out for (see the photograph on page 2).

Serves 4

1 x 400ml (14 fl oz) can of coconut milk
300ml (10 fl oz) Oriental Stock (see page 28), or stock made with a cube
450g (1 lb) cauliflower florets
250g (9 oz) thread egg noodles
2 teaspoons sesame oil
55g (2 oz) spinach, roughly shredded
100g (3½ oz) cashew nuts, toasted
salt and black pepper
oil for deep-frying

For the Thai paste:
2 dried chillies, soaked in boiling water for 5 minutes
1 lemongrass stalk, finely chopped
2 garlic cloves, roughly chopped
5cm (2 inch) piece of fresh root ginger, peeled and chopped
1 tablespoon coriander seeds
2 tablespoons vegetable oil
4 tablespoons roughly chopped coriander, with stalks
1 fresh red chilli, de-seeded
zest of 1 lime

1 Place all the Thai paste ingredients in a blender or small food processor and whizz together. (This can be done the day before, and kept in the fridge.) Transfer the paste to a wok or large pan and fry for 2 minutes.

2 Add the coconut milk and stock to the fried paste, and bring to the boil. Add the cauliflower florets and simmer for 8–10 minutes until just cooked.

3 Meanwhile, cook the noodles separately, as directed on the packet, and drain. Toss half of the noodles in the sesame oil and set to one side.

4 Add the spinach to the broth and simmer for a further minute. Stir in the warm cashew nuts. Season to taste if necessary.

5 Deep-fry the remaining noodles, in two batches, in hot oil for 1–2 minutes, until crisp.

6 To serve, pile the sesame-dressed noodles into four serving bowls, and ladle over the Thai broth. Break each batch of crisp deep-fried noodles into two and place on top of the broth. Serve at once.

> ⓥ **Two raw chicken breasts, cut into thin strips, can be used in place of the cauliflower at stage 2.**

Apple Pasta Pesto Soup

This warming, rustic soup, thick with pasta and vegetables, is finished with a generous dollop of fresh pesto.

S e r v e s 4

2 tablespoons olive oil
2 large Bramley cooking apples, peeled, cored and diced
2 leeks, shredded
3 sun-dried tomatoes, chopped
1 sun-dried red pepper, sliced
1 garlic clove, crushed
1 × 400g (14 oz) can of chopped tinned tomatoes
a pinch of sugar
1 bay leaf
850ml (1½ pints) Root Vegetable Stock (see page 29), or stock made with a cube
115g (4 oz) small dried pasta cylinder shapes
115g (4 oz) string or dwarf beans, trimmed
salt and black pepper
4 tablespoons Fresh Pesto (see page 23)

1 In a large saucepan heat the olive oil. Add the apple and the leek and cook for 5 minutes, until lightly browned.

2 Add the sun-dried tomato and pepper, garlic, canned tomatoes, sugar, bay leaf and stock. Bring the contents of the pan to the boil and simmer for 20 minutes.

3 Add the pasta and beans and season well. Simmer for a further 10–12 minutes or until the pasta is cooked (adding extra stock if needed).

4 Ladle the soup into large soup bowls and top with a spoonful of pesto sauce. Serve with plenty of crusty bread.

Taking Your **PULSE**

I have a passion for pulses and I use them a great deal. They're inexpensive, versatile, satisfying and store well. Also, like staples, they're great flavour absorbers.

Take your pulse and cook it in many different ways. Make a warming stew as in the Spring Bean and Garlic Zuppa, or a warm Chickpea Pistou salad; try mean-tasting Borlotti Bean Burgers, or a tasty bean butter topped with rocket.

The overnight soak is not always necessary, especially in the case of lentils. Check individual packets for instructions. And remember that beans and lentils can be bought ready cooked, in cans, and are an excellent alternative, especially if you prefer a slightly softer texture.

Eating pulses with grains makes for a good source of protein (see A Word on Health, page 8) which is essential in vegetarian cookery. An example of this is the Spicy Rice and Beans on page 76, which is further enhanced by the yoghurt in the accompanying raita.

Whatever your pulse rate, these beans are definitely broader!

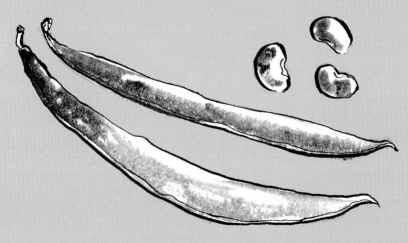

Spring Bean and Garlic Zuppa

This gutsy soup is more like a light stew than a soup.
Serve with hunks of granary bread.

Serves 4

olive oil
3 garlic cloves, crushed
225g (8 oz) dried split butter beans, soaked overnight and drained
1 tablespoon roughly chopped fresh parsley
1 tablespoon roughly chopped fresh thyme
1 tablespoon roughly chopped fresh rosemary
1 bay leaf
150ml (5 fl oz) white wine
1.2 litres (2 pints) Root Vegetable Stock (see page 29), or stock made with a cube
salt and black pepper
115g (4 oz) spring greens, finely shredded
2 tablespoons grainy mustard
fresh rosemary to garnish

1 In a large saucepan heat 1 tablespoon of the oil. Add the garlic and gently fry for 30 seconds.

2 Add the drained butter beans, herbs, wine and stock and season well. Boil the soup for 10 minutes, then reduce to a simmer for a further 5–10 minutes, until the beans are just cooked. Add the spring greens 5 minutes before the end of the cooking time.

3 Just before serving, stir in the mustard, and taste to check the seasoning. Then ladle the soup into warm soup bowls and finish with a drizzle of olive oil, some freshly ground black pepper, and fresh rosemary.

Spicy Rice and Beans

This is wonderfully warming fodder. The mango and mint raita is an absolute must, and gives this dish an extra edge.

Serves 4

2 tablespoons sunflower oil
1 large onion, chopped
2 garlic cloves, crushed
2 fresh red chillies, de-seeded and chopped
1 tablespoon medium curry paste
225g (8 oz) long-grain rice
1 × 400g (14 oz) can of kidney beans, drained
1 × 400g (14 oz) can of black-eye beans, drained
about 850ml (1½ pints) Root Vegetable Stock (see page 29), or stock made with a cube
salt and black pepper
115g (4 oz) frozen petits pois
2 tablespoons roughly chopped fresh parsley

To serve:
1 quantity Mango and Mint Raita (see page 12)

1 In a large saucepan or wok heat the oil and fry the onion for 5 minutes until golden brown. Add the garlic, chilli and curry paste, then stir in the rice. Cook for a further minute.
2 Mix in the beans, pour in 500ml (18 fl oz) of the stock, and season well. Bring the contents of the saucepan to the boil, cover and simmer for 25–30 minutes or until the rice is cooked, adding extra stock if needed.
3 Add the *petits pois* for the final 5 minutes of the cooking time.
4 Pile the steaming hot rice and beans into warm serving dishes and scatter over the parsley. Serve with the raita.

Spiced Gingered Lentils

Serve these more-ish lentils topped with bhaji-like crispy onions or on baked sweet potatoes.

Serves 4

1 tablespoon olive oil
2 leeks, shredded
2 teaspoons garam masala
2.5cm (1 inch) piece of fresh root ginger, peeled and grated
250g (9 oz) green lentils, washed and drained
850ml (1½ pints) Oriental Stock (see page 28), or stock made with a cube
salt and black pepper

To serve:
2 tablespoons Greek-style yoghurt
Crispy Onions (see page 113)
2 tablespoons chopped fresh coriander
lime wedges

1 In a saucepan heat the oil and fry the leeks gently for 5 minutes. Add the garam masala and ginger and cook for 1 minute.

2 Add the lentils and stock and bring to the boil. Simmer for 30–35 minutes or until the lentils are just cooked (adding extra stock or water if the pan becomes too dry). Season to taste.

3 Spoon the curried green lentils on to four large dinner plates. Drizzle over some yoghurt and top each serving with some crispy onions, coriander and a lime wedge.

> ⓥ **The crispy onions can be replaced by grilled fish.**

Broad Bean and Rocket Salad on White Bean Butter

A speedy, rich bean butter, which is great just as a dip or as a pâté spread on crusty bread or garlic toast.

Serves 4

175g (6 oz) fresh or frozen broad beans, cooked and peeled
2 teaspoons walnut oil
40g (1½ oz) rocket leaves
salt and black pepper
lemon wedges to garnish

For the white bean butter:
2 × 425g (15 oz) cans of butter beans, drained and rinsed
4 teaspoons creamed horseradish
5 tablespoons olive oil
juice and zest of 1 lime
3 tablespoons warm water

1 Make the bean butter first. In a food processor or liquidiser, whizz together the butter beans, creamed horseradish, olive oil, lime juice and zest and warm water until smooth and creamy. Season well.

2 In a bowl, toss the peeled, bright green broad beans with the walnut oil. Add the rocket leaves and gently toss again.

3 Divide the creamy pâté between four dinner plates and scatter the bean and rocket salad over. Grind over plenty of black pepper, and serve with the lemon wedges and warm crusty bread.

> ⊗ Instead of the rocket and broad beans, serve the butter bean pâté with roast beef.

Borlotti Bean Burgers

A taste of the Med, burger style. Serve on a good Italian-style bread with a generous amount of basil mayo.

Serves 4

55g (2 oz) pine kernels

1 × 425g (15 oz) can of borlotti beans, drained, rinsed and thoroughly dried on kitchen paper

½ red onion, finely chopped

1 tablespoon sun-dried tomato paste

55g (2 oz) fresh breadcrumbs

1 egg, beaten

salt and black pepper

sunflower oil for frying

To serve:

ciabatta or country-style bread

salad leaves

a little Basil Mayo (see page 25)

1 In a hot frying pan, lightly toast the pine kernels for 2–3 minutes until golden. Set to one side.

2 Place the borlotti beans in a large bowl and, using a fork, mash well. Add the onion, sun-dried tomato paste, half the breadcrumbs, the beaten egg and the pine kernels and combine, seasoning to taste with salt and pepper.

3 Divide the mixture into four and shape into four flat burgers. Coat the outside of each burger with the remaining breadcrumbs. Place in the fridge for 1 hour.

4 Heat 1cm (½ inch) of sunflower oil in a large frying pan and add the burgers. Fry for 3–4 minutes on each side until golden and drain on kitchen paper.

5 Serve the burgers immediately on lightly toasted ciabatta bread topped with salad leaves. Spoon some basil mayo over each burger.

Cannellini and Walnut Butter with Pan-fried Vegetables

This fluffy bean butter makes a fantastic partner for the pan-fried vegetables.

Serves 4

550g (1¼ lb) selected vegetables (i.e. sugar-snap peas, small carrots halved lengthwise, asparagus tips)
1 tablespoon olive oil
juice of ½ lemon
salt and black pepper

For the butter:
2 × 400g (14 oz) cans of cannellini beans, drained and rinsed
3 tablespoons walnut oil
2 tablespoons olive oil
75ml (2¾ fl oz) water
2 teaspoons lemon juice

1 Make the butter first. Place all the ingredients in a food processor and whizz until smooth. Season well with salt and pepper. Set to one side.

2 Plunge the vegetables into a large pan of boiling water for 30 seconds. Remove and plunge into iced water to quickly cool, before draining well.

3 In a large frying pan or wok, heat the olive oil. Add the drained vegetables and stir-fry briefly for about 1–2 minutes until heated through. Squeeze over the lemon juice and season.

4 To serve, pile the cannellini bean butter on to a large serving dish and spread out slightly to form a base. Spoon over the hot vegetables and serve at once with warm crusty bread.

Garlic Dhal

Serve these spicy lentils with Fragrant Orange Rice (see page 63) and a cooling Date and Coriander Raita to come to the rescue (see page 12).

Serves 4–6

1 tablespoon sunflower oil
1 large onion, chopped
4 garlic cloves, crushed
1 tablespoon ground turmeric
1 tablespoon garam masala
6 cardamom pods, crushed
1 bay leaf
350g (12 oz) orange lentils, washed
about 850ml (1½ pints) Root Vegetable Stock (see page 29), or stock made with a cube
salt and black pepper
225g (8 oz) fresh spinach leaves, roughly chopped

1 In a large saucepan heat the oil and fry the onion for 5–6 minutes until golden brown. Stir in the garlic, turmeric, garam masala, crushed cardamom pods and bay leaf. Fry gently for 1 minute until lightly toasted.

2 Add the lentils and stock and season well. Simmer for approximately 15–20 minutes or until the lentils are just tender.

3 Stir in the chopped spinach and cook for a further 5 minutes.

Puy Lentils with Coconut and Lime

The coconut milk adds a delicious richness to these tiny, tender Puy lentils. Serve with Flat Flapjack Raisin Bread (see page 97) and Red Onion and Coriander Salsa (see page 13).

Serves 4

1 tablespoon olive oil
1 large onion, chopped
1 garlic clove, crushed
2 fresh red chillies, de-seeded and finely chopped
5cm (2 inch) piece of fresh root ginger, peeled and grated
450g (1 lb) Puy lentils
1.2 litres (2 pints) Oriental Stock (see page 28), or stock made with a cube
200ml (7 fl oz) carton of coconut cream
grated rind and juice of 1 lime

1 In a large saucepan, heat the oil and fry the onion for 5 minutes. Add the garlic, chilli and ginger and fry for a further minute.

2 Stir in the lentils and most of the stock and bring to the boil. Boil for 10 minutes, then reduce the heat and simmer for a further 20 minutes or until the lentils are cooked, adding more liquid if necessary.

3 Stir in the coconut cream, lime rind and juice, and gently heat through.

> Ⓥ **These lentils make an interesting accompaniment to roast pork.**

Chickpea Pistou

A lively and tasty way to serve up chickpeas. If you like a bit of crunch, cook them as in the recipe; for a softer texture, use canned chickpeas (2 × 400g/14 oz tins, drained and rinsed).

Serves 4

175g (6 oz) dried chickpeas, soaked overnight and drained
150ml (5 fl oz) olive oil
1 red onion, cut into thick slices
2 large carrots, peeled and diced
2 garlic cloves, crushed
2 fresh red chillies, de-seeded and finely chopped
1 teaspoon ground cumin
1 teaspoon ground coriander
150ml (5 fl oz) white wine
juice of 1 lemon
4 plum tomatoes, cut into small wedges
1 large bunch of fresh flat-leaf parsley
salt and black pepper

1 Place the chickpeas in a saucepan and cover with water. Bring to the boil and simmer for 1–1½ hours or until just tender. Allow to cool in the cooking liquid until required.

2 In a saucepan, heat 1 tablespoon of the olive oil and gently fry the onion and carrot for 10 minutes until softened. Add the garlic, chilli, cumin and coriander, and cook for a further 30 seconds. Pour in the wine and simmer for 5 minutes.

3 Transfer the spiced onion and carrot to a large mixing bowl and combine with the drained chickpeas, lemon juice, tomato and parsley. Season well and leave to marinate for at least 2 hours.

4 Serve with toasted garlic bread or grilled polenta.

> ⓥ **Add 115g (4 oz) chopped garlic sausage with the garlic and spices.**

Upper CRUST

This chapter contains recipes dedicated to carbohydrates in the form of flour-based foods. It features a stylish range of simple tarts, pizzas, galettes, pies and breads.

Try instant garlic and flavour-spiked breads or delectable upside-down-style pies. The pies can all be made using good-quality bought pastry, or try my Butter Pastry Crust, which is easier than pie!

Bread is often assumed to be far too much bother to make. But many of these recipes make use of modern-day conveniences, like instant pizza dough mix, which with a few cheeky additions can be transformed into skillet-pan pizzas or a rosemary crust for charred vegetables.

Stylish doesn't mean difficult. The Roquefort Galette on page 90 uses a simple brioche dough recipe, and the end result is outstanding!

Butter Pastry Crust

Hit the switch, it's as simple as that! Use this instead of any bought shortcrust pastry.

Makes 450g (1 lb) pastry

280g (10 oz) plain flour
a pinch of salt
140g (5 oz) butter (unsalted or slightly salted), diced
2 egg yolks
2 tablespoons cold water

1 Simply place all the ingredients in the processor, and whizz until the ingredients just come together. Beware not to *over*process.

2 Refrigerate until required. Make life easy for yourself, and before chilling, pat the butter pastry dough into a rough circle the size of a large side plate. Wrap and chill. This makes the pastry chill much more quickly, and it's also easier to roll out when it comes back to room temperature.

Regular Prune Pie

Robust, rich and ravishingly good. An upside-down pie, rather like a savoury tatin, although you could make mini versions for individual servings. If goat's cheese isn't your thing, you could use a cream cheese instead.

Serves 4

2 tablespoons olive oil
15g (½ oz) butter
2 large red onions, thinly sliced
16 pre-soaked prunes, halved lengthways
140g (5 oz) mild goat's cheese
salt and black pepper
2 tablespoons fresh thyme leaves
225g (8 oz) puff pastry
extra thyme or salad leaves to garnish

1 Preheat the oven to 220°C/425°F/Gas Mark 7.

2 In a saucepan heat the olive oil and butter together, and cook the onion gently until softened and lightly coloured.

3 Lightly grease a 20cm (8 inch) diameter non-stick cake tin with a little olive oil. Arrange 10 of the prune halves in the base. Dot a little goat's cheese and some softened red onion in the gaps and set to one side.

4 Mix the remaining onion, cheese and prunes together and season well. Carefully add this mixture to the tin, taking care not to disturb the arrangement on the bottom of the tin. Scatter with thyme leaves.

5 Roll out the pastry to about 5mm (¼ inch) thick and cut out a circle 20cm (8 inches) in diameter. Place the pastry in the tin, very lightly tucking the edges inside the tin.

6 Bake in the oven for 15–20 minutes, until the pastry is risen and cooked. Turn upside down to turn out, so the pastry becomes the base of the tart. Garnish with fresh thyme or salad leaves, and serve hot or warm.

Polish Pasty

A delicious loaf stuffed with a vegetable and cheese filling, which is wonderful served with Baked Tomato Chutney (see page 21) or a simple green salad.

Serves 4–6

450g (1 lb) bought puff pastry
1 egg, beaten

For the filling:
175g (6 oz) new potatoes, scrubbed
1 small Savoy cabbage, finely shredded
25g (1 oz) butter
140g (5 oz) feta cheese, diced
115g (4 oz) cherry tomatoes, halved
½ bunch of fresh thyme
salt and black pepper

1 In a large pan of boiling water, cook the new potatoes for 10–12 minutes, until just cooked. Meanwhile, steam the cabbage until just tender, and drain very well.

2 Melt the butter in a saucepan and toss with the potatoes, cabbage, feta cheese, tomatoes and thyme leaves. Season well, and set to one side.

3 Preheat the oven to 220°C/425°F/Gas Mark 7.

4 Roll out the pastry on a floured surface into a large round about 35cm (14 inches) in diameter, and place on a baking sheet. Put the cabbage mixture on one half of the round. Brush the edges of the pastry with the beaten egg and fold over to form a large pasty shape, sealing the edges together. Brush again with beaten egg and decorate with any excess pastry trimmings.

5 Bake in the preheated oven for 30–35 minutes or until the pastry is golden brown and cooked, reducing the heat if the top becomes too brown. To serve, place on a wooden chopping board and cut into thick slices.

Roquefort Galette

The best bread and cheese you're ever likely to eat!
Serve on its own or with Cranberry Salsa (see page 16).

Serves 4

For the brioche:
350g (12 oz) plain flour
a pinch of salt
2 teaspoons sugar
1 sachet easy-blend yeast
approx. 50ml (2 fl oz) warm water
2 eggs, beaten
85g (3 oz) unsalted butter, melted and cooled slightly

For the topping:
100g (3½ oz) Roquefort cheese
2 tablespoons sweet white wine
2 tablespoons roughly chopped sage leaves
25g (1 oz) unsalted butter
1 beaten egg, for glaze

1 In a large bowl, combine the flour, salt, sugar, yeast and enough warm water to form a soft dough. Make a well in the centre and add the eggs and melted butter.

2 Knead lightly until smooth. Place the dough in a clean bowl, cover and leave in a warm place to prove for about 1–1½ hours until it has doubled in size.

3 When it has risen, 'knock back' by kneading the dough again for 5 minutes.

4 Take half of the brioche and roll it out into a rough circle about 23cm (9 inches) in diameter. Transfer to a lightly greased baking sheet. Divide the remaining dough into 10 pieces and roll each piece into a ball. Using a little glaze as glue, evenly place these balls in a circle on the brioche forming a wall around the border. Cover and leave in a warm place to prove until the balls are slightly risen and almost touching.

5 Preheat the oven to 220°C/425°F/Gas Mark 7.

6 Crumble the cheese over the brioche, within the wall, and spoon over the wine. Scatter over most of the sage and knobs of butter. Brush dough with beaten egg.

7 Bake in the preheated oven for 15 minutes. Reduce the heat to 190°C/375°F/Gas Mark 5 and cook for a further 10 minutes or until the brioche is golden and cooked through and the cheese melted and bubbling. Scatter with the remaining sage leaves and serve at once.

Skillet Pizza with Caramelised Apples and Feta

No-fuss instant pizzas which take only minutes to cook.

Serves 4

1 × 280g (10 oz) packet of white pizza dough mix
2 garlic cloves, crushed
200ml (7 fl oz) hand-hot water
4 tablespoons olive oil

For the topping:
55g (2 oz) unsalted butter
2 dessert apples, cored and thickly sliced
2 teaspoons sugar
½ quantity Raw Tomato Salsa (see page 13)
225g (8 oz) feta cheese, roughly crumbled
4 fresh basil sprigs

1 In a large bowl, combine the pizza dough mix with the garlic and water. Bring together to form a dough and divide the dough into 4 pieces. Knead each piece of dough on a lightly floured surface until smooth and springy. Roll out each piece of dough into a circle about 13cm (5 inches) in diameter and set to one side.

2 In a large frying pan, heat 2 tablespoons of the olive oil. Place two of the pizza bases in the oil and cook over a gentle heat for 2–3 minutes on each side, until puffed up and golden. Repeat with the remaining bases in the remaining oil. Drain well.

3 Meanwhile, in a frying pan, heat the butter for the topping until foaming, toss in the apple slices and sprinkle with the sugar. Fry the apple slices for 4–5 minutes, until golden and caramelised.

4 To serve, place each pizza on a serving plate and spoon on a little tomato salsa. Top the salsa with some caramelised apples and feta cheese. Garnish each with a sprig of basil and serve at once.

> ⓥ **Replace the feta cheese with 55g (2 oz) prosciutto, torn into strips.**

Charred Peppers with a Rosemary Crust

Roasted vegetables have become very popular these days. The rosemary bread topping makes a great cooking lid, and is a wonderful accompaniment for the peppers.

Serves 4

3 tablespoons olive oil
1 orange pepper, de-seeded and cut into quarters
1 yellow pepper, de-seeded and cut into quarters
1 red pepper, de-seeded and cut into quarters
4 garlic cloves
1 large red onion, cut into thin wedges
1 bay leaf
a pinch of sugar
salt and black pepper

For the crust:
1 × 150g (5½ oz) packet of white pizza dough mix
1 tablespoon chopped fresh rosemary
olive oil
rock salt

1 Preheat the oven to 220°C/425°F/Gas Mark 7.
2 Pour the oil into a large, shallow baking dish and place the dish in the oven to heat up for 10 minutes.
3 Remove the dish from the oven and place in it the peppers, garlic, onion and bay leaf. Sprinkle over the sugar and season well.
4 Return the dish to the oven and cook the vegetables for about 30–35 minutes or until lightly charred.
5 Meanwhile, make up the bread dough as per the instructions on the packet, adding the chopped rosemary. Knead well and allow to stand for 10–15 minutes.
6 Roll the dough out thinly, until the size of the baking dish. Cover the charred vegetables with the dough and prick the top of the dough with a fork.
7 Brush the dough with some olive oil and scatter over some rock salt. Return the dish to the oven and bake for a further 15–20 minutes or until the bread is golden and crisp.
8 To serve, invert the dish on a plate and turn out, with the crust on the bottom and the vegetables on top. Serve at once.

Tomato Scofa Bread

Really quick and easy, and excellent made with dill and caraway seeds (see the variation below).

Serves 4

225g (8 oz) plain flour
a pinch of salt
3 level teaspoons baking powder
black pepper
about 150ml (5 fl oz) milk
4 sun-dried tomatoes in oil, drained and chopped
2 tablespoons sun-dried tomato oil
2 tablespoons chopped fresh chives

1 Preheat the oven to 220°C/425°F/Gas Mark 7.

2 Sift the flour, salt and baking powder into a large bowl. Grind in some black pepper.

3 In a large jug, gently combine the milk, sun-dried tomato, sun-dried tomato oil and chives. Add this to the flour and baking powder and gently combine to form a soft and manageable dough (adding extra milk if necessary).

4 On a lightly floured surface, roll the dough out to roughly 2.5cm (1 inch) thick. Form into a round about 15cm (6 inches) in diameter. Mark the round of dough into six triangles with a knife, taking care not to cut all the way through the dough. (For individual breads, cut the dough into eight rounds with a 5cm/2 inch round cutter.)

5 Cook the large bread in the preheated oven for 12–15 minutes (the individual ones for 6–7 minutes) until risen and golden brown.

Dill and Caraway Scofa Bread

Omit the sun-dried tomato oil, sun-dried tomato and chives, and replace with 2 tablespoons olive oil, 1 teaspoon caraway seeds (lightly crushed), and 2 tablespoons roughly chopped fresh dill.

Walnut Bread

*Good as it is or serve with Roquefort cheese and
Apple and Walnut Marmalade (see page 20).*

Serves 6–8

225g (8 oz) strong white flour
225g (8 oz) malted granary flour
a pinch of salt
1 sachet easy-blend yeast
150ml (5 fl oz) warm milk
1 egg, beaten
1 tablespoon olive oil
100–150ml (3–5 fl oz) warm water
225g (8 oz) shelled walnuts
beaten egg to glaze

1 Sift the flours and salt into a large bowl. Stir in the yeast. Make a well in the centre of the flour and stir in the warm milk, beaten egg, olive oil and enough of the water to form a soft, wet dough.

2 On a lightly floured surface, knead the dough for 10 minutes, until smooth and elastic.

3 Place the dough in a lightly oiled large bowl. Cover and leave to prove in a warm place for about 1 hour, until doubled in size.

4 When the dough has risen, knead it again to 'knock it back' and gradually incorporate the walnuts, until well distributed throughout the dough. Shape the dough into one large or two smaller rounds, as required. Place on a lightly floured baking sheet and slash the top of each loaf. Cover the loaf (loaves) and return to a warm place until risen by about half again.

5 Meanwhile, preheat the oven to 220°C/425°F/Gas Mark 7.

6 Glaze the loaves with beaten egg and bake in the preheated oven for 10–15 minutes, then reduce the heat to 190°C/375°F/Gas Mark 5, and bake for a further 15 minutes for a smaller loaf, or 30 minutes for the larger. The loaves are cooked when they are risen and golden and sound hollow when tapped underneath.

7 Cool on a wire rack.

Flat Flapjack Raisin Bread

This easy bread makes a great accompaniment to cheese, soups, stews and salads – or is good just on its own. Eat it on the day you cook it.

Serves 4–6

115g (4 oz) porridge oats
2 teaspoons baking powder
115g (4 oz) plain flour
115g (4 oz) raisins or sultanas
2 tablespoons roughly chopped fresh thyme
1 small onion, grated
1 egg
1 level teaspoon salt
black pepper
125ml (4 fl oz) milk
3 tablespoons olive oil

1 Preheat the oven to 200°C/400°F/Gas Mark 6.

2 In a large bowl mix together all the ingredients except the olive oil. The mixture will be quite wet, like a very thick batter.

3 Place a baking tray containing 2 tablespoons of the olive oil in the preheated oven and heat for 5 minutes. Spread the wet dough on to the hot baking tray and shape into a rough round, about 15–18cm (6–7 inches) in diameter. Brush the remaining oil over the top.

4 Return the tray to the oven for 20 minutes, then flip the bread over and continue to bake for a further 6–8 minutes, or until brown.

5 Remove the bread from the oven and allow it to cool for a few minutes, then cut it into wedges and serve warm. (Re-heat the bread in the oven if it has cooled.)

Garlic Doorsteps

These rustic-style hunks of garlic bread are quicker, less expensive, and far more delicious than any ready-made version. Opposite they are topped with tasty Hot Olive Pâté (see page 36).

Serves 4

4 thick-cut slices of country bread
2 garlic cloves, peeled
2 tablespoons virgin olive oil
2 tablespoons roughly chopped fresh parsley
freshly ground black pepper

1 Preheat the grill.

2 Toast the bread doorsteps on both sides.

3 Remove from the grill and while hot, rub with the garlic cloves. Drizzle over the olive oil and sprinkle with the chopped parsley. Season with black pepper and eat immediately.

Mini Hazelnut Scones Topped with Avocado Mayo

These nutty scones can be served hot and buttered to go with soups, stews or cheese. If you can't be bothered to make them, serve the creamy avocado mayo on mini oatcakes or cut-out small rounds of toasted buttered bread, or simply serve it as a dip.

Makes 16 mini scones (or 8 larger)

225g (8 oz) plain or granary flour
1 tablespoon baking powder
a pinch of salt
55g (2 oz) butter
55g (2 oz) chopped hazelnuts
150ml (5 fl oz) milk

To serve:
Avocado Mayo (see page 24)
1 teaspoon paprika

1 Preheat the oven to 220°C/425°F/Gas Mark 7. Lightly flour a baking tray.
2 Sift the flour, baking powder and salt into a mixing bowl. Rub in the butter until the mixture resembles fine breadcrumbs. Stir in the nuts and milk and, using a fork, lightly combine the ingredients together to form a soft dough.
3 Transfer the dough to a lightly floured surface and knead very lightly. Using your hands press out to a thickness of about 2.5cm (1 inch). Using a fluted 4cm (1½ inch) cutter, cut out 16 small rounds.
4 Place the scones on the floured baking sheet, and bake in the preheated oven for 8–10 minutes, or until risen and lightly browned. Transfer to a wire rack to cool.
5 To serve, cut each scone in half and fill each with a spoonful of avocado mayo. Replace the tops and lightly sprinkle each with a little paprika. Serve at once.

Spiced Croûtes

A spicy alternative to garlic bread, these croûtes *are delicious for mopping up gutsy juices.*

Serves 4–6

1 teaspoon each of paprika, ground cumin and ground coriander
black pepper
3 tablespoons olive oil
55g (2 oz) unsalted butter
1 small baguette, sliced

1 In a small bowl, combine all the spices together. Grind in some black pepper.

2 In a large frying pan, heat the olive oil and the butter. Stir in the spices, then add the slices of baguette.

3 Fry the bread until golden brown on each side. Drain on kitchen paper and serve at once.

Squash, ROOT and Fruit

Gone are the days when cooking vegetables meant throwing them into a pan of boiling water. Now, the care and forethought that were once given to preparing meat and fish at long last have been applied to the humble vegetable.

Squashes such as marrows, courgettes and pumpkins are often considered tasteless, watery and, in some cases, much too large to deal with. This is a real shame, as once prepared and baked, their flavour becomes concentrated and the vegetable is transformed. Try the light citrus taste of the Orange-basted Marrow or Baked Whole Pumpkin which makes a great accompaniment and looks magnificently impressive.

Root vegetables are robust, and they also lend themselves well to being roasted, mashed or, at their best, combined with spices, garlic and mustard as in Spicy Parsnips and Carrots or Hot Celeriac Rémoulade.

The aubergine, known as the vegetarian steak, is classed as a fruit vegetable and it has a wonderful capacity for absorbing flavour. Not only can it be baked or grilled, but it can also be turned into delectable pâtés and gentle curries.

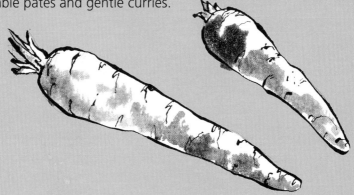

Spicy Parsnips and Carrots

Parsnips and carrots have a subtle, sweet flavour, which works well with the butter and spices. Serve with a cooling mint raita.

Serves 4

450g (1 lb) medium parsnips, peeled and quartered
450g (1 lb) medium carrots, peeled and halved
55g (2 oz) unsalted butter, melted
1 tablespoon sunflower oil
salt and black pepper
1 teaspoon coriander seeds
1 teaspoon cardamom pods, crushed
1 bay leaf
1 teaspoon cumin seeds
6 black peppercorns
1 teaspoon hot paprika
1 cinnamon stick

1 Preheat the oven to 200°C/400°F/Gas Mark 6.

2 In a large pan of boiling water, parboil the parsnips and carrots for 8 minutes. Drain well.

3 Place the vegetables in a roasting tin with the butter and oil. Toss together and season well.

4 Roast the vegetables in the preheated oven for 20–25 minutes or until golden and crisp.

5 Meanwhile, place all the spices in a pestle and mortar and grind together.

6 After 20–25 minutes, remove the vegetables from the oven and sprinkle with the ground spices. Toss the vegetables with the spices and return to the oven for a further 8–10 minutes. Serve at once with a mint raita.

Aubergine and Apple Ragoût with Cheese and Mustard *Croûtes*

An upmarket Welsh rarebit with a Mediterranean twist, these cheese and mustard croûtes can also be served with soups and stews or on a crisp green salad.

Serves 4

For the ragoût:
1 tablespoon olive oil
1 onion, thickly sliced
1 red pepper, de-seeded and cut into thick strips
2 garlic cloves, chopped
1 aubergine, cut into bite-sized chunks
1 courgette, thickly sliced
85ml (3 fl oz) red or white wine
175ml (6 fl oz) tomato passata
2 dessert apples, cored and thinly sliced
salt and black pepper
1 bunch of fresh basil

For the *croûtes:*
4 thick slices of country-style bread
butter
85g (3 oz) mature Cheddar cheese, grated
85g (3 oz) Gruyère cheese, grated
2 tablespoons grainy mustard
3 tablespoons beer

1 For the ragoût, in a saucepan heat the olive oil and fry the onion and pepper gently for 5 minutes. Add the garlic, aubergine and courgette and fry for a further 5 minutes.

2 Add the wine to the pan and simmer for 2 minutes. Then add the passata and sliced apples and season well. Cover the saucepan and simmer for a further 8–10 minutes or until the apples have softened slightly but still hold their texture and shape.

3 Meanwhile, for the *croûtes*, preheat the grill and lightly toast the bread on each side. Butter generously. In a small bowl mix together the cheeses with the mustard and beer. Spread this equally over each piece of buttered toast and return to the grill until bubbling hot and golden.

4 To serve, place the cheesy-mustard *croûtes* on to four warm dinner plates. Spoon a generous heap of the ragoût to one side, and decorate each plate with a large sprig of fresh basil. Serve at once.

> ⓥ **Instead of the cheese and mustard *croûtes*, serve the ragoût with a pork chop or gammon steak.**

Dry Spice Aubergine Oven Curry

The dry spice marinade works magic when roasted with the aubergines, which are then finished with creamy coconut milk and masses of coriander. Serve with Fragrant Orange Rice (see page 63) and warm naan bread. You could cook courgettes in the same way.

Serves 2

2 medium aubergines, diced
1 quantity Dry Spice (see page 27)
1 × 400ml (14 fl oz) can of coconut milk
3 tablespoons roughly chopped fresh coriander

1 Preheat the oven to 190°C/375°F/Gas Mark 5.

2 Toss the aubergine in the dry spice and transfer to an ovenproof dish.

3 Bake the aubergine in the preheated oven for 25–30 minutes, or until it is lightly charred and tender.

4 Pour the coconut milk over the spiced aubergine and return to the oven until bubbling hot, about 8–10 minutes.

5 Scatter over the coriander and serve at once.

Hot Celeriac Rémoulade

OK, bite the bullet and peel this root, it's truly worth the effort, with its pungent celery flavour and root vegetable texture.

Serves 4 as a starter or 2 as a main course with bread and salad

2 × 450g (1 lb) celeriac heads, peeled and cut into 2.5cm (1 inch) thick wedges
4 tablespoons olive oil
juice of 1 lemon
salt and black pepper

For the dressing:
1 tablespoon grainy mustard
3 tablespoons Greek-style yoghurt

To serve:
1 bunch of fresh chives, roughly chopped

1 Preheat the oven to 220°C/425°F/Gas Mark 7.
2 Place the celeriac in a shallow ovenproof dish. Toss with the oil and lemon juice and season well.
3 Roast in the preheated oven for 35–40 minutes, until lightly charred and just tender.
4 Meanwhile, combine the dressing ingredients together, season and set to one side.
5 To serve, arrange a few wedges of celeriac on each plate. Dollop a generous spoonful of dressing on top and finish with a sprinkling of chives. Serve at once.

Hot Beetroot and Dill with Soured Cream

Excellent with Dill and Caraway Scofa Bread (see page 95), beetroot, dill and soured cream marry superbly together – a lively way to serve the much under-rated beetroot. If you can't be bothered to make the bread (which is easy), serve on a large buttered baked potato.

Serves 4

425g (15 oz) raw beetroot
55g (2 oz) butter
1 bunch of fresh dill, roughly chopped
salt and black pepper
juice and zest of 1 lemon
175ml (6 fl oz) soured cream (or fromage frais)

1 Peel the beetroot and shred it through the food processor or hand grate it on a coarse grater.
2 In a large frying pan, melt the butter. Toss the beetroot in the butter and stir-fry for 2 minutes until very hot. Stir in 2 tablespoons of the roughly chopped dill.
3 Season with salt, black pepper, lemon juice and zest.
4 Serve immediately topped with soured cream and garnished with more dill.

> ⊗ **This hot beetroot can be served on its own, or with the soured cream, as a side vegetable for pan-fried salmon.**

Pesto Cobbler with Parsnips

A hearty parsnip stew, generously flavoured with paprika and with a hint of pesto, home-made or bought.

Serves 4

1 tablespoon sunflower oil
1 large onion, chopped
225g (8 oz) red peppers, de-seeded and sliced
900g (2 lb) parsnips, peeled and coarsely chopped
1 garlic clove, crushed
2 tablespoons paprika
2 teaspoons plain flour
1 × 400g (14 oz) can of chopped tomatoes
1 tablespoon tomato purée
900ml (1½ pints) Root Vegetable Stock (see page 29), or stock made with a cube
1 tablespoon fresh thyme leaves
1 bay leaf
salt and black pepper

For the pesto cobbler:
85g (3 oz) plain flour
¼ teaspoon salt
½ level teaspoon baking powder
¼ teaspoon bicarbonate of soda
55g (2 oz) cornmeal or fine semolina
100g (3½ oz) natural yoghurt
1 large egg, beaten
25g (1 oz) butter, melted
1 tablespoon Fresh Pesto (see page 23)
40g (1½ oz) Parmesan cheese, grated

1 Preheat the oven to 200°C/400°F/Gas Mark 6.
2 In a large saucepan or frying pan, heat the oil. Add the onion and red pepper and fry for 6–7 minutes until softened and golden. Add the parsnip, garlic and paprika and fry for a further minute.
3 Sprinkle over the flour and cook for a further minute, then add the chopped tomato, tomato purée, stock, thyme and bay leaf. Season well with salt and pepper.
4 Transfer the stew to a shallow ovenproof dish and place in the preheated oven for 35 minutes.

5 Meanwhile, in a large mixing bowl, stir together the flour, salt, baking powder and bicarbonate of soda. Stir in the cornmeal or semolina and set to one side. In a smaller bowl, beat together the yoghurt, egg and melted butter.

6 Lightly combine the yoghurt mixture with the dry ingredients, then briefly fold in the pesto. Take care not to over-mix; the pesto should still be in streaks.

7 Remove the stew from the oven 12 minutes before the end of the cooking time and place dessertspoonfuls of the pesto cobbler on top. Sprinkle over the grated Parmesan and return the stew to the oven for the final 12 minutes' cooking, or until the cobblers are risen and golden brown and the stew is bubbling hot.

> ⊗ Replace the parsnips with 8 skinless, boneless chicken thighs, cut into chunks. Add at stage 2 with the garlic and paprika.

Orange-basted Marrow

The delicate flavour of the orange marinade transforms this summer squash dish. It is great served on Basil Butter Bulgar (see page 58).

Serves 4

1 small marrow, about 900g (2 lb) in weight
1 quantity Orange and Shallot Marinade (see page 27)
salt and black pepper
55g (2 oz) whole almonds, roughly chopped
2 tablespoons chopped fresh flat-leaf parsley

1 Peel the marrow and cut in half lengthwise. Scoop out the seeds, then cut each half in half widthways to create four boats.

2 Toss the marrow in the marinade and allow to soak for an hour.

3 Preheat the oven to 220°C/425°F/Gas Mark 7.

4 Place the marrow with the juices in a large, shallow, ovenproof dish. Spoon the shallot into the marrow shells and season well.

5 Bake in the preheated oven for 50–60 minutes. About 5 minutes before serving, sprinkle the almonds and parsley over the marrow and return to the oven until the almonds are lightly roasted. Serve at once.

Aubergine and Tomato *Croûte*

Garlic croûtes *topped with a smooth aubergine pâté and piquant hot tomatoes.*

Serves 4

1 small granary French stick
olive oil
450g (1 lb) ripe plum tomatoes, roughly chopped
1½ tablespoons red wine vinegar
2 tablespoons chopped fresh basil
salt and black pepper

For the aubergine pâté:
2 medium aubergines
1 slice of brown bread
3 garlic cloves, crushed
juice of ½ lemon
1 tablespoon chopped fresh parsley
4 tablespoons virgin olive oil

1 Preheat the oven to 200°C/400°F/Gas Mark 6.
2 Prick the aubergines with a fork several times and place them on a lightly oiled baking sheet. Bake in the preheated oven for 35–40 minutes until the skins are wrinkled and the flesh is soft.
3 Soak the bread slice in a little water and squeeze out. Set to one side.
4 Cut the aubergines in half lengthways and, using a spoon, scoop out the flesh from the skin. Place the aubergine flesh in a food processor with the bread, garlic, lemon juice, parsley and olive oil, and whizz until smooth and creamy. Season well with salt and pepper.
5 Cut the French bread into four thick diagonal slices and lightly brush with a little olive oil. Bake in the oven (same temperature as above) for 6–8 minutes until lightly toasted.
6 Meanwhile, heat 1 tablespoon olive oil in a small frying pan, add the tomatoes and toss over a high heat for 30 seconds. Pour in the vinegar, add the basil and season to taste.
7 Remove the *croûtes* from the oven and top each with a generous portion of the aubergine pâté. Place the *croûtes* on a large platter or four individual serving plates. Spoon the hot tomatoes with all their juices over the *croûtes*, and serve at once.

> ⊗ **This aubergine pâté makes a great accompaniment to roast leg of lamb.**

Onion Gratin

*Outrageously rich but good! Serve with country-style bread
and a crisp green salad.*

Serves 4

900g (2 lb) onions, peeled and cut in half through the root
25g (1 oz) butter
225g (8 oz) spinach, washed and coarsely shredded
salt and black pepper
freshly grated nutmeg
1 heaped teaspoon ground turmeric
1 teaspoon ground cumin
300ml (10 fl oz) double cream
25g (1 oz) fresh breadcrumbs

1 In a large pan of boiling water, boil the onion halves for 30–35 minutes, until just tender. Drain well on kitchen paper.

2 Preheat the oven to 220°C/425°F/Gas Mark 7.

3 Meanwhile, in a saucepan heat the butter until foaming, toss in the spinach, and cook for 2–3 minutes until wilted. Season well with black pepper, a little salt and a grating of nutmeg. Transfer the spinach to the base of a large, shallow, ovenproof dish.

4 Separate the onion layers slightly and arrange on top of the spinach.

5 Heat a small frying pan and add the turmeric, cumin and ¼ teaspoon nutmeg. Toast the spices for 30 seconds before stirring into the cream.

6 Pour the spiced cream over the onions and sprinkle over the breadcrumbs. Bake in the preheated oven for 20 minutes until the top is golden and the gratin bubbling hot.

Crispy Onions

*Serve on salad leaves for a light supper
or with the Spiced Gingered Lentils on page 77 for a heartier dish.*

Serves 4

2 eggs
2 teaspoons garam masala
115g (4 oz) self-raising flour
about 150ml (5 fl oz) water
1 bunch of spring onions, finely chopped
1 large red onion, finely sliced
salt and black pepper
vegetable oil for frying

1 In a large bowl, beat the eggs. Add the garam masala, flour and water and mix well.
Stir in the onions and season to taste.

2 In a large sauté or frying pan, heat 2cm (¾ inch) vegetable oil until a bread cube sizzles
when dropped into the fat.

3 Divide the mixture into eight. Lift up using a tablespoon and a fish slice, and slide four
portions at a time into the hot fat. Fry over a medium heat for 6–7 minutes on each side,
then drain on kitchen paper. Repeat with the remaining mixture to make another four
bhaji-like crispy onion cakes.

Aubergine Steaks with Olive and Raisin Gravy

These marinated aubergine steaks are delicious served with the Nectarine Relish on page 19.

Serves 4

2 medium aubergines
salt and black pepper
250g (9 oz) mozzarella cheese, sliced
lamb's lettuce for serving

For the marinade:
4 tablespoons olive oil
juice of ½ lemon
1 garlic clove, crushed

For the gravy:
2 tablespoons olive oil
6 shallots, halved
a pinch of sugar
2 garlic cloves, crushed
150ml (5 fl oz) red wine
150ml (5 fl oz) port
6 each of green and black olives, pitted
175g (6 oz) raisins
1 bay leaf
1 large fresh thyme sprig

1 Cut each aubergine into four long tongues, by slicing lengthways. In a bowl combine all the marinade ingredients and season with black pepper. Pour over the aubergine steaks and leave to marinate for 30 minutes.

2 For the gravy, in a saucepan, heat the olive oil and add the shallots and sugar. Sauté for 10 minutes until golden. Stir in the garlic, red wine, port, olives, raisins, bay leaf and thyme and season well. Bring the gravy to the boil and simmer for 2 minutes. Cover the pan with a lid and simmer for a further 20 minutes.

3 Meanwhile, preheat the grill to medium.

4 Place the aubergine tongues on a baking sheet and grill for 5–6 minutes on each side.

5 Top the flesh side of each tongue with a slice of mozzarella cheese and return to the grill for a further 4–5 minutes until the cheese is melted and slightly browned.

6 Place a small pile of lamb's lettuce on each serving plate. Top with two of the aubergine steaks and accompany with a serving of the olive and red wine gravy.

> Ⓥ **This gravy works well with grilled or fried lamb steaks.**

Aubergine Terrine

Simply baked aubergines, stacked with soured cream and salsa – mouthwatering and very striking.

Serves 4

4 medium aubergines, cut into 8mm (⅓ inch) thick slices
4 tablespoons olive oil
salt and black pepper
1 quantity Raw Tomato Salsa (see page 13)
4 tablespoons soured cream
2 tablespoons fresh mint leaves, roughly chopped

1 Preheat the oven to 220°C/425°F/Gas Mark 7.

2 Place the aubergine slices and olive oil in an ovenproof dish. Toss together and season well. Bake the aubergine in the preheated oven for 20–25 minutes, until just softened and lightly golden. Set to one side to cool.

3 To assemble the terrine, place a layer of the aubergine slices, overlapping, on the base of a large serving dish. Spoon over some of the raw tomato salsa and a little soured cream. Continue to layer upwards in this way with all of the aubergine. Finish with a final layer of salsa and soured cream.

4 Scatter over the mint, and serve at room temperature.

Fried Plantain with Raw Tomato Salsa

Plantain is a banana which must be cooked. It is made into plantain chips in the Caribbean, and here they are served with a chilli salsa for dipping (or an avocado mayo, see page 24).

Serves 2

2 green plantains
vegetable oil for frying
salt and black pepper

To serve:
sugar
1 quantity Raw Tomato Salsa (see page 13)

1 Remove the plantain skins and slice the flesh at an angle into thin slices.
2 Pour 2.5cm (1 inch) of vegetable oil into a large, deep frying pan. Heat the oil until it sizzles when a bread cube is dropped in.
3 Fry half of the plantain slices in the oil for 1–2 minutes until golden brown. Remove with a slotted spoon and drain on kitchen paper. Repeat with the remaining plantain slices.
4 To serve, sprinkle over a little sugar or salt to taste, and serve with the salsa as a dip.

Baked Whole Pumpkin

Pumpkins are plentiful in the autumn. Make the most of them in soups, or sliced and roasted with olive oil or, best of all, baked as here. Serve to accompany Spiced Gingered Lentils (see page 77) with Crispy Onions (see page 113), or the Fragrant Orange Rice on page 63.

Serves 2–3

1 pumpkin, about 15cm (6 inches) in diameter
25g (1 oz) butter, softened
salt and pepper
freshly grated nutmeg
1 large fresh rosemary sprig

1 Preheat the oven to 190°C/375°F/Gas Mark 5.

2 Cut a lid from the stalk end of the pumpkin and pull out the fibre and seeds.

3 Spread the softened butter inside the pumpkin and season really well with the salt, pepper and nutmeg. Place the rosemary sprig inside and replace the lid.

4 Place the pumpkin on a large ovenproof dish and bake for 45–50 minutes in the preheated oven or until the flesh is soft.

5 Serve the pumpkin whole, allowing each person to scoop out their own portion.

Red Fire Ragoût

A hot and spicy tomato ragoût, which is wonderful served on or between the Herb Polenta Slabs on page 60, and of course with pasta.

Serves 4

2 tablespoons olive oil
2 red peppers, halved, de-seeded and thickly sliced
1 orange pepper, halved, de-seeded and thickly sliced
1 bunch of spring onions, halved and sliced lengthways into strips
4 cardamom pods, crushed
2 fresh red chillies, de-seeded and finely chopped
1 garlic clove, crushed
150ml (5 fl oz) white wine
1 × 400g (14 oz) can of cherry tomatoes
12 Greek black olives, pitted
1 tablespoon small capers
salt and black pepper

1 In a frying pan heat the oil and gently fry the red and orange peppers for 5 minutes until softened. Add the spring onion, cardamom, chilli and garlic and fry for a further minute.

2 Pour in the white wine and simmer for 3 minutes. Then add the cherry tomatoes, black olives and capers and season well. Simmer over a gentle heat for 2–3 minutes, and serve at once.

> ⊗ Replace the red peppers with 225g (8 oz) prepared squid, thickly sliced, adding it at the end of stage 1.

Fungus MUNGUS

Mushrooms come in many shapes and forms – fresh, dried or preserved in oil or brine. These flavoursome fungi are tremendously versatile and in these recipes are roasted, flamed and grilled.

Classic garlic mushrooms, instead of being deep-fried, are given a twist by being baked on a crust and finished with lashings of garlic butter. Potatoes and shallots are enlivened by wild mushrooms to form a rich, rustic stew.

Mushrooms are now so in vogue that whole books have been dedicated to them. If I had to choose my own personal favourite, it would be that monstrous, black, flat field mushroom. It's not necessarily the prettiest, but it's always full of flavour and never disappointing. Use it to make mushroom broth, or fry whole and serve on spinach polenta with a lemon kick!

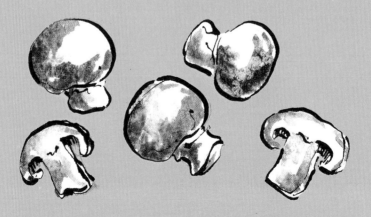

Wild Mushroom and Fennel Pies

A tasty mushroom stew baked under a puff pastry crust,
which I encountered on a trip to Finland.

Serves 4

15g (½ oz) dried wild mushrooms
55g (2 oz) butter
1 leek, washed and shredded
1 fennel bulb, finely sliced
1 medium celeriac head, peeled and cut into fine strips
juice of 1 lemon
115g (4 oz) chestnut mushrooms, sliced
salt and black pepper
4 tablespoons white wine
350ml (12 fl oz) double cream
4 tablespoons chopped fresh chives
450g (1 lb) ready-rolled puff pastry
1 egg, beaten

1 Soak the dried mushrooms in water as directed on the packet, then set to one side.

2 In a large frying pan, melt the butter and fry the leek, fennel and celeriac for 5–6 minutes.

3 Add the lemon juice, and stir in the fresh sliced mushrooms. Fry for a further 4 minutes, then season well and allow to cool slightly. Preheat the oven to 200°C/400°F/Gas Mark 6.

4 Drain the dried mushrooms and add to the vegetables with 2 tablespoons of the soaking liquid. Spoon this mixture into four ovenproof soup bowls or small pie dishes.

5 Combine the wine with the cream and season well. Divide this equally between the filled dishes, and top each with a tablespoon of chopped chives.

6 On a lightly floured surface, roll out the pastry a little and cut out four pastry lids slightly larger than the soup bowl tops. Brush the edges of the pastry lids with beaten egg and lay over the top of each dish, pressing and sealing well round the sides. Brush the pastry tops all over with the remaining beaten egg and place the pies on a baking tray.

7 Bake for 15–18 minutes or until the pastry is puffed up and golden brown.

> ⊗ **115g (4 oz) of very thinly sliced salmon can be used in place of the chestnut mushrooms. Do not pre-fry the salmon, just add with the dried mushrooms at stage 4.**

Mushroom Broth with Buttermilk Mash and Spicy Cabbage

A creamy bowl of mushroom soup topped first with the buttermilk mash, the 'bubble', and then the 'squeak', some dark green cabbage. If you can't be bothered to make the mash, you could add some cooked pasta, perhaps tossing it in with the cabbage.

Serves 4

25g (1 oz) unsalted butter
450g (1 lb) chestnut mushrooms, wiped and thickly sliced
350g (12 oz) flat field mushrooms, wiped, peeled and thickly sliced
115g (4 oz) button mushrooms, wiped
2 heaped teaspoons plain flour
150ml (5 fl oz) dry sherry
300ml (10 fl oz) Bouquet Garni Stock (see page 29), or stock made with a cube
1 bunch of fresh thyme, roughly chopped
salt and black pepper
200ml (7 fl oz) double cream
a squeeze of lemon juice

For the spicy cabbage:
1 tablespoon olive oil
1 large leek, washed and shredded
450g (1 lb) dark green cabbage or spring greens, washed and finely shredded
freshly grated nutmeg

To serve:
1 quantity Buttermilk Mash (see page 68)

1 In a large frying pan or wok, heat the butter and fry the three varieties of mushroom until slightly softened, about 5 minutes.

2 Sprinkle over the flour and cook for 1 minute. Add the sherry, half the stock, and the thyme. Season well and simmer for 10–15 minutes.

3 Meanwhile, in a large frying pan or wok, cook the cabbage. Heat the olive oil and fry the leek briskly for 2 minutes. Add the shredded cabbage and stir-fry over a high heat for 2–3 minutes or until limp and just tender. Season with nutmeg, salt and pepper to taste. Keep warm.

4 Warm through the mashed potato.

5 Add the cream and lemon juice to the mushroom broth, and simmer for a further 5 minutes, adding extra vegetable stock if the broth looks too thick. (The broth should be like a thick gravy.)

6 To serve, ladle the broth into four warmed, large soup plates. Place a scoop of creamy mashed potato in the centre of the broth and top this with a flourish of spicy cabbage. Hand the remaining mashed potato and cabbage separately.

Garlic Mushroom Splats

Mushrooms baked on an onion bread crust, and smothered with garlic butter just before serving. Fabulous!

Serves 4

1 × 150g (5½ oz) packet of white pizza dough mix
salt and black pepper
350g (12 oz) small field mushrooms, peeled and trimmed, with stalks on
1 tablespoon olive oil
1 tablespoon chopped fresh flat-leaf parsley

For the onion parsley:
1 medium red onion, roughly chopped
2 tablespoons chopped fresh flat-leaf parsley

For the garlic butter:
55g (2 oz) butter, softened
1 garlic clove, crushed

1 Preheat the oven to 220°C/425°F/Gas Mark 7.

2 In a large bowl, make up the pizza dough as directed on the packet. Knead well, cover and set to one side.

3 In a small food processor or blender make the onion parsley. Whizz together the red onion and parsley, and season well with salt and pepper. Set to one side.

4 Divide the pizza dough into four and roll out each piece into a rough splat of about 15cm (6 inches) in diameter. Place on a baking sheet and top each splat with some onion parsley, leaving a border around the outside. Crowd the mushrooms, stalk side up, on top of the onion parsley.

5 Brush the mushrooms and edges of the dough with a little olive oil and bake in the preheated oven for 10–12 minutes until the bases are golden and crisp.

6 Meanwhile, combine the butter and the crushed garlic, and season well with salt and pepper.

7 Remove the mushroom splats from the oven and immediately top each mushroom stalk with a blob of garlic butter. Sprinkle with parsley and serve at once.

Marinated Mushrooms with Basil Pistou on Brioche

Posh mushrooms on toast!

Serves 4

4 large flat mushrooms, peeled and trimmed
salt and black pepper
2 brioche buns, halved and toasted
Parmesan cheese shavings to serve

For the marinade:
150ml (5 fl oz) olive oil
50ml (2 fl oz) balsamic vinegar

For the basil pistou:
50ml (2 fl oz) virgin olive oil
2 garlic cloves, roughly chopped
1 large bunch of fresh basil
a squeeze of lemon juice

1 In a jug, combine the olive oil with the balsamic vinegar and season well with salt and pepper. Pour the marinade over the flat mushrooms and set to one side for 30 minutes.
2 Preheat the grill to medium.
3 In a small food processor, place the virgin olive oil, garlic and basil for the pistou and whizz to combine. Season with the lemon juice, salt and pepper and set to one side.
4 Grill the mushrooms for 6–7 minutes on each side or until just cooked. Baste the mushrooms with any excess marinade as they cook.
5 To serve, place half a toasted brioche bun on each plate and top with a grilled mushroom, stalk side up. Shave some Parmesan over the hot mushroom and surround the bun with a drizzle of basil pistou. Serve at once.

Spaghettini with Flamed Mushrooms and Green Peppercorns

Green peppercorns are an unripe, softer and hence not as powerful, version of the black peppercorn. Sold mostly preserved in brine, they should be rinsed well before using.

Serves 4

115g (4 oz) sugar-snap peas, topped
55g (2 oz) unsalted butter
1 onion, chopped
450g (1 lb) button mushrooms, wiped
2 tablespoons brandy
200ml (7 fl oz) crème fraîche
2 tablespoons green peppercorns
a squeeze of lemon juice
salt and black pepper
350g (12 oz) spaghettini pasta

1 Bring a large pan of water to the boil. Plunge in the sugar-snap peas and simmer for 1 minute. Drain the peas and plunge immediately into a bowl of cold water to cool. Drain well and then, using a small sharp knife, cut the peas in half by slicing vertically down their length. Set to one side.

2 In a large pan, heat the butter. Add the onion and fry for 5 minutes. Add the mushrooms and fry for a further 7–8 minutes.

3 Meanwhile, cook the pasta as directed on the packet.

4 In a ladle, carefully heat the brandy. Ignite the brandy and pour over the mushrooms in the pan.

5 Allow the flames to burn out, then add the *crème fraîche* and peppercorns, and season with the lemon juice, salt and pepper. Simmer for a further 2 minutes, stir in the sugar snaps and heat through for another minute or until everything is piping hot.

6 Place a serving of pasta on each plate. Spoon over the mushroom and peppercorn sauce and serve at once.

Potato and Forest Mushroom Ragoût

A robust, richly flavoured stew, based on a recipe from the south-west of France.

Serves 4

55g (2 oz) butter
175g (6 oz) shallots, peeled and halved
1 teaspoon soft brown sugar
115g (4 oz) shiitake mushrooms
115g (4 oz) mixed wild mushrooms
3 whole garlic cloves, unpeeled
675g (1½ lb) Charlotte potatoes, scrubbed and cut in half lengthways
150ml (5 fl oz) white wine
150ml (5 fl oz) Bouquet Garni Stock (see page 29), or stock made with a cube
1 bay leaf
1 fresh rosemary sprig
salt and black pepper
175g (6 oz) baby leaf spinach

1 In a large, heavy-based pan, heat the butter and add the shallots and sugar. Fry for 4–5 minutes until golden brown.

2 Add the mushrooms and the garlic and fry for a further 3 minutes.

3 Add the potatoes, wine, stock, bay leaf and rosemary, and season well. Bring to the boil, cover and simmer for 20–30 minutes until just cooked.

4 Remove the lid and increase the heat slightly. Cook for a further 5 minutes, to evaporate some of the liquid and give the ragoût a shiny glaze.

5 To serve, pile some baby spinach leaves on to four serving plates or bowls. Spoon over the ragoût with its pan juices, and serve at once.

> Ⓧ **Use 25g (1 oz) of goose fat in place of the butter. Replace 115g (4 oz) of the mushrooms with the same amount of bacon lardons. These can be added with the mushrooms and garlic at stage 2.**

Spinach Polenta with Saucy Lemon Mushrooms

One of my favourite ways of flavouring that hearty Italian staple without the use of Parmesan!

Serves 4

For the mushrooms:
4 very large flat mushrooms
1 garlic clove, crushed
2 teaspoons mushroom ketchup
3 tablespoons sweet sherry
juice and rind of 1 lemon
1 bunch of fresh thyme
black pepper
40g (1½ oz) unsalted butter

For the spinach polenta:
225g (8 oz) quick-cook instant polenta
1 litre (1¾ pints) Bouquet Garni Stock (see page 29), or stock made with a cube
115g (4 oz) fresh spinach, roughly chopped
55g (2 oz) butter
freshly grated nutmeg
salt and black pepper

1 In a bowl, combine the garlic, mushroom ketchup, sherry, lemon juice and rind and 2 tablespoons of thyme leaves. Add the mushrooms and grind over some black pepper. Set to one side.

2 Place the stock in a large pan and bring to the boil. Gradually pour in the polenta, stirring continuously. Add the spinach and stir over the heat for 1 minute until the polenta is thick and the spinach wilted. Stir in the butter. Season well with freshly grated nutmeg, salt and pepper.

3 In a large frying pan, melt the unsalted butter. Add the mushrooms with all their marinade and fry for 5–6 minutes, turning once.

4 To serve, place a mound of spinach polenta on each plate and top each mound with a flat mushroom. Spoon over the pan juices, garnish with the remaining thyme leaves and serve at once.

Baked Mushrooms in Tarragon Herb Paste

Serve these mushrooms on Garlic Doorsteps (see page 98).
Wild mushrooms are good, but chestnut or button can be used as well.

Serves 4 as a starter

225g (8 oz) shiitake mushrooms, wiped
225g (8 oz) mixed wild mushrooms, wiped
1 quantity Tarragon Herb Paste (see page 26)

1 Preheat the oven to 200°C/400°F/Gas Mark 6.

2 Toss the mushrooms in the tarragon paste and transfer the mushrooms with the paste into a large ovenproof dish or roasting tin.

3 Bake in the preheated oven for 15–20 minutes, and serve hot.

In **PRAISE** of Pudding

Puddings have come a long way from being a dish solely designed to fill an Englishman's stomach and keep out the cold. This traditional type of pudding has not been overlooked here (see Cinnamon and Orange Plum Pudding), and with the introduction of vegetarian suet, can now be cooked by all, meat-eaters and vegetarians alike.

However, the following chapter also contains recipes that carry influences from all over the world, from a Greek-inspired baklava to Thai bananas in syrup with a salted coconut custard.

But whatever and wherever you're cooking, not many would disagree with Monsieur Misson when he said 'Blessed be he that invented the pudding!'

Panettone and Apricot Maple Pudding

A delicious instant pudding, made in a flash.

Serves 4

175g (6 oz) dried pre-soaked apricots
juice of 2 oranges
2 large bananas, peeled and thickly sliced
40g (1½ oz) unsalted butter
3 tablespoons pure maple syrup
1 teaspoon ground cinnamon
4 thick-cut slices of panettone, or 2 currant buns, halved
225g (8 oz) mascarpone cheese
4 tablespoons crème fraîche
icing sugar for dusting

1 Place the apricots and orange juice in a saucepan and simmer for 5–6 minutes until the apricots have softened. Add the bananas and simmer for a further 2 minutes.

2 Heat the butter and maple syrup with the cinnamon in a large frying pan. Add the panettone slices (or halved buns, cut side down), and cook for about 5 minutes until golden brown.

3 Meanwhile, in a bowl, beat the mascarpone cheese with the *crème fraîche* and set to one side.

4 Lift the panettone or bun halves on to four large serving plates and drizzle over any remaining syrup and butter. Top with the cheese mixture and spoon over a generous portion of the warm fruit. Dust each portion with icing sugar and serve at once.

Cider-baked Coxes with a Maize Crust

Rich, aromatic apples, baked with cider. Apple pie was traditionally served with a hunk of cheese; here the cheese is combined with polenta in the pastry to make a wonderful butter crust. Serve with vanilla ice-cream.

Serves 6

For the pastry:
115g (4 oz) plain flour
55g (2 oz) quick-cook instant polenta
a pinch of salt
115g (4 oz) butter
15g (½ oz) Gruyère cheese, finely grated
1 small egg, beaten
caster sugar for sprinkling

For the filling:
6 Coxes or small dessert apples, peeled, cored and halved
55g (2 oz) unsalted butter, melted
150ml (5 fl oz) fruity cider
25g (1 oz) soft brown sugar
1 fresh rosemary sprig

1 Preheat the oven to 200°C/400°F/Gas Mark 6.

2 Into a large bowl, sieve the flour, polenta and salt. Rub in the butter until the mixture resembles fine breadcrumbs. Stir in the cheese and enough egg to bind the dough together. Chill the dough for 30 minutes.

3 Place the apples in a shallow, round, ovenproof dish about 23cm (9 inches) in diameter. Combine the melted butter with the cider, and pour over the apples. Sprinkle the apples with the brown sugar and tuck in the sprig of rosemary.

4 On a lightly floured surface, roll out the pastry until it is large enough to lie as a blanket over the apples. Carefully lift the pastry over the apples; roughly trim the edges and tuck inside the dish. Lightly sprinkle the pastry with caster sugar.

5 Bake the pie for 10 minutes, then reduce the oven temperature to 180°C/350°F/ Gas Mark 4. Bake for a further 30–35 minutes until the apples are softened and cooked. Serve hot.

Honey and Hazelnut Baklava with Cardamom Cream

Layers of crisp filo pastry, filled with honey, apples and hazelnuts. The cardamom cream can be served with other desserts, with pies and fresh fruit.

Serves 4

55g (2 oz) butter
200g (7 oz) filo pastry
100g (3½ oz) hazelnuts, chopped and lightly roasted
3 Coxes or small dessert apples, cored and sliced
115g (4 oz) clear honey
85ml (3 fl oz) water

For the cardamom cream:
300g (10½ oz) Greek-style yoghurt
1 teaspoon clear honey
4 cardamom pods, crushed
juice of ½ orange

1 Preheat the oven to 190°C/375°F/Gas Mark 5.

2 Melt the butter and use a little of it to grease a large non-stick baking sheet.

3 Lay one sheet of filo pastry on the base of the tray and brush generously with melted butter. Cover with a further three sheets of filo, buttering well between each addition.

4 Scatter the chopped nuts and a layer of apple slices over the filo and cover with a further three sheets of buttered filo pastry. Sprinkle over the remaining nuts and apples and place a further three layers of buttered filo pastry to fit the top. Using a sharp knife, mark the top layer of the baklava into diamond shapes.

5 Bake in the preheated oven for 35 minutes until golden brown.

6 Meanwhile, in a saucepan, heat the honey with the water and simmer for 5 minutes. Set to one side to cool slightly.

7 When the baklava is cooked, remove it from the oven and spoon over the honey syrup. Allow the baklava to cool before removing it from the baking tray. Serve on a large platter.

8 For the cardamom cream, simply mix all the ingredients together and serve.

Flat Blueberry Tart

A stunning-looking tart that requires very little effort, combining fresh fruit, cream cheese and pastry. Blueberries are not the only fruit – try fresh apricots, peaches or strawberries, to name but a few.

Serves 6–8

350g (12 oz) shortcrust pastry
caster sugar for rolling
280g (10 oz) cream cheese
juice and grated rind of 1 large orange
2 tablespoons icing sugar
280g (10 oz) blueberries
icing sugar for dusting

1 Preheat the oven to 200°C/400°F/Gas Mark 6. Line a baking tray with non-stick baking parchment.

2 On a clean surface, using caster sugar in place of flour, roll out the pastry until approximately 5mm (¼ inch) thick. Using a large dinner plate, cut out a neat round about 23cm (9 inches) in diameter and carefully place on to the lined baking tray. Prick the pastry all over and crimp or fork the edges.

3 Bake the pastry in the oven for 10–12 minutes, or until cooked and biscuit coloured. Allow the pastry to cool completely before carefully transferring to a serving plate.

4 In a small bowl beat the cream cheese with the orange juice and grated rind, adding icing sugar to taste. Spread this mixture over the pastry base leaving a 2.5cm (1 inch) border clear.

5 Top the orange cream with the blueberries and lightly dust with icing sugar. Serve at once.

Sticky Coconut Rice

This recipe is inspired by the Orient. Serve it with fresh mango, or go one stage further and try it with Caramelised Spicy Fruits (see opposite, and the photograph on page 7).

Serves 4

225g (8 oz) Thai fragrant rice
85g (3 oz) caster sugar
1 cinnamon stick
1 × 400ml (14 fl oz) can of coconut milk

1 In a large pan of boiling water, cook the fragrant rice for 10 minutes.
2 Drain the rice well and return to the saucepan. Add the sugar and cinnamon stick and stir in the coconut milk. Return the pan to the heat, cover and simmer for 10–12 minutes or until all the coconut milk has been absorbed.
3 To serve, place a disc of greaseproof paper in the base of a 1.2 litre (2 pint) or individual pudding basins. Spoon the rice into the bowl, and allow to stand, cool and 'gel' together for 30 minutes.
4 Turn the rice out on to a serving dish, and serve immediately with its fruit accompaniment.

Espresso Ice-cream Cup

The combination of the very strong coffee and the melting cold ice-cream topped with grated chocolate and cinnamon makes a sensational coffee iced cream. Eat with a spoon then drink! (If you don't have an espresso coffee-maker, use some good, strong coffee from a cafetière or filter.)

Serves 2

4 scoops traditional vanilla ice-cream
300ml (10 fl oz) espresso coffee, freshly brewed
25g (1 oz) bitter Continental chocolate, grated
icing sugar and cinnamon for sprinkling

1 Divide the ice-cream between two extra large coffee cups.
2 Pour over some freshly made espresso coffee to almost cover the ice-cream and top with a sprinkling of grated chocolate.
3 Finish with a light dusting of cinnamon and icing sugar and eat at once!

Caramelised Spicy Fruits

These hot and aromatic grilled fruits make an exciting change from standard fruit salad. They are good with the coconut rice opposite.

Serves 4

1 large ripe mango
½ fresh ripe pineapple, cored, peeled and thickly sliced
2 bananas, peeled and halved lengthways
1 ripe paw-paw, seeded and cut into 4 wedges

For the spicy butter:
85g (3 oz) unsalted butter
5cm (2 inch) piece of fresh root ginger, peeled and finely chopped
2 teaspoons icing sugar
juice and grated zest of 1 lime

1 To prepare the mango, cut a thick slice from either side of the large flat stone that runs through the centre of the fruit. With a small, sharp knife, make diagonal cuts through the flesh, in a lattice fashion, taking great care not to cut through to the skin. Cut each slice in half lengthways and push the skin up to open out the lattice cuts.

2 Preheat the grill to its highest setting. Place the prepared fruits on a baking tray, flesh side up.

3 In a small saucepan, melt the butter and add the ginger and icing sugar. Remove from the heat and stir in the lime juice and zest. Brush the fruits liberally with the spicy butter.

4 Grill the fruits for 6–7 minutes, until caramelised and bubbling hot. Serve at once.

Vanilla Pears with Toasted Brioche

*Pears are always around, but they usually seem to be poached for pudding.
Here they are pot-roasted in a lovely vanilla syrup.*

Serves 4

6 small ripe dessert pears
1 vanilla pod
115g (4 oz) granulated sugar
1 piece of lemon rind
85ml (3 fl oz) water
25g (1 oz) unsalted butter, cubed
2 brioche buns
juice of ½ lemon
4 dessertspoons crème fraîche *or Greek-style yoghurt*

1 Preheat the oven to 200°C/400°F/Gas Mark 6.

2 Peel, halve and core the pears, leaving the stalks on. Arrange them in a shallow ovenproof dish.

3 Split the vanilla pod and toss around in the sugar.

4 Scatter 85g (3 oz) of the sugar over the pears. Add the lemon rind and vanilla pod and pour the water in between the pears. Scatter over the butter.

5 Bake the pears in the preheated oven for 20–25 minutes until just soft.

6 Preheat the grill. Cut each brioche bun into two rounds, and lightly toast them on both sides.

7 Remove the pears from the oven, sprinkle with the remaining sugar, and grill until lightly browned and slightly crisp. Squeeze over the lemon juice.

8 To serve, place the brioche toasts on four plates. Top each with a dessertspoon of *crème fraîche* or yoghurt. Carefully place three pear halves over the cream and drizzle with the vanilla syrup. Serve at once.

Morello Cherry Mess

The richness of the pudding contrasts greatly with the sour morello cherries (which can be bought in jars, in syrup). Do not substitute the morellos with sweet black cherries; instead try raspberries, blackberries or orange segments.

Serves 4

225g (8 oz) Greek-style yoghurt
150ml (5 fl oz) double cream, lightly whipped
4 small meringue nests, broken into bite-sized pieces
1 large jar morello cherries, drained
100g (3½ oz) dark chocolate

1 In a large bowl, simply fold the yoghurt, cream and meringue pieces together, then gently add the drained cherries.
2 Melt the dark chocolate in a bowl over a pan of simmering water.
3 Spoon the morello cherry mess into large serving glasses and top with the melted chocolate.

Exotic Iced Fruits with Rum

An easy, refreshing cheat's ice-cream. The fruits should be cut into even-sized pieces to ensure the best result (or you can buy chopped ready-to-use exotic fruit in bags in some supermarkets).

Serves 6–8

1 small pineapple
1 large ripe mango or 2 ripe paw-paws
½ Galia melon
1 tablespoon icing sugar, or to taste
4–5 tablespoons rum
150ml (5 fl oz) double cream

1 Cut the pineapple, mango and melon into rough 3cm (1¼ inch) pieces. Place in a shallow, freezer-proof container, and freeze until nearly frozen.
2 Transfer the nearly frozen fruit to a large food processor. Briefly whizz together with the icing sugar, rum and double cream. The iced fruits should be blended but not runny.
3 Serve at once or return to the freezer until required.

Cinnamon and Orange Plum Pudding

No hours of steaming required, just fill, roll and bake for a wonderful, wicked, warming, winter pudding. The Apple and Walnut Marmalade on page 20 can replace the Plum Marmalade.

Serves 4–6

225g (8 oz) self-raising flour
225g (8 oz) vegetarian suet
1 heaped teaspoon ground cinnamon
a pinch of salt
grated zest of 1 orange
cold water to mix
icing sugar and cinnamon for dusting

For the filling:
1 quantity Plum Marmalade (see page 21)

For the sauce:
500g (1 lb 2 oz) Greek-style yoghurt
100g (3½ oz) frozen concentrated orange juice, thawed

1 Preheat the oven to 200°C/400°F/Gas Mark 6. Line a baking sheet with non-stick baking parchment.

2 In a large bowl, mix together the flour, suet, cinnamon, salt and orange zest. Stir in enough water to form a dough.

3 On a lightly floured surface, roll the dough out into a rough 30cm (12 inch) square. Transfer the pastry on to the non-stick baking parchment.

4 Pile the plum marmalade on to half of the suet pastry, wet the pastry edges and fold over to encase the marmalade.

5 Bake in the preheated oven for 25–30 minutes until the pastry is crisp and brown.

6 Meanwhile, make the sauce. In a small bowl, simply combine the yoghurt with the orange juice.

7 To serve, using the non-stick baking parchment to help you, transfer the pudding to a large serving dish. Dust with the icing sugar and cinnamon and serve warm with the orange yoghurt sauce.

Bananas in Syrup with Coconut Custard

Yes, it's not a mistake, there is a little salt in the coconut custard!
The result is surprisingly good, not to be missed.

Serves 4

12 apple bananas, or 5 small bananas, peeled

For the syrup:
600ml (1 pint) water
225g (8 oz) granulated sugar
3 star anise
1 piece of orange rind
4 passionfruit, scooped out

For the coconut custard:
1 × 400ml (14 fl oz) can of coconut milk
1 teaspoon cornflour
1 dessertspoon cold water
a pinch of salt

1 Place all the syrup ingredients, except for the passionfruit, in a saucepan over a low heat and stir until the sugar has dissolved. Increase the heat and boil the syrup until it has halved in volume.

2 Place the bananas in the syrup and simmer for 6–8 minutes, until they are just cooked, but still holding their shape.

3 Meanwhile, in a small pan, heat the coconut milk until simmering. In a small bowl dissolve the cornflour in the water. Stir the cornflour mix into the coconut milk and simmer, stirring, for 1 minute. Stir in the salt.

4 To serve, stir the passionfruit pulp into the banana syrup. Spoon the bananas and syrup on to four dessert plates, and finish with a serving of warm coconut custard.

Cooking Up a SPREAD

A special occasion doesn't necessarily mean loads of people. This chapter contains recipes for special occasions when you're entertaining any number, from four to twelve people, from small picnics, to drinks and nibbles, to formal suppers and large gatherings.

Large or small, the most important point is 'less is more'. From the daunting Christmas lunch to the banquet buffet, it's far better to concentrate on a few great dishes that eat well together, which you too can enjoy.

For a formal supper-style buffet, serve the Alpine Pasta and Crisp Vegetable Black Bean Strudel with hot bread and a green salad, or try one or all of the continental pies on pages 143–4. Or for going out, the Provençal Buttie, Sugar-snap Pea Tart with Ginger Pistou and Big Coleslaw are excellent travellers.

For a modern-day cheese and wine party, try the Hot Ploughman's Dip with some Walnut Bread and celery, Hot Brie and Apple Tart or Blue Brie with Plum Marmalade. And if time is really short, a loaf of crusty bread, a wedge of good cheese, some ripe pears and a jug of wine go a long way.

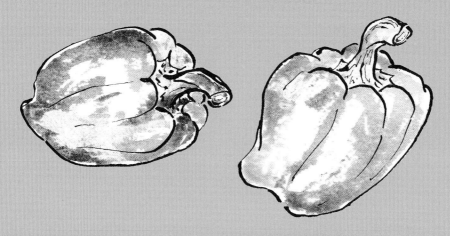

Spinach, Ricotta and Pine Kernel Pie

*This continental-style pie has masses of flavour,
as do the two alternative fillings that follow.*

Serves 4–6

450g (1 lb) shortcrust pastry
1 egg yolk mixed with 1 tablespoon water

For the filling:
1 tablespoon olive oil
1 small red onion, finely sliced
225g (8 oz) spinach leaves, shredded
225g (8 oz) ricotta cheese
25g (1 oz) toasted pine kernels
freshly grated nutmeg
salt and black pepper

1 Preheat the oven to 200°C/400°F/Gas Mark 6.

2 On a lightly floured surface, roll out half of the pastry into a rectangle of about 20 × 25cm (8 × 10 inches). Transfer to a baking sheet and relax in the fridge for 10 minutes.

3 Prick the pastry base all over with a fork and bake in the preheated oven for 12–15 minutes, until golden brown. Remove from the oven and allow to cool.

4 Meanwhile, heat the oil for the filling in a pan and fry the onion for 5–6 minutes until lightly browned and softened. Stir in the spinach, then immediately transfer the onion and spinach to a bowl. Add the ricotta, pine kernels and a grating of nutmeg. Season well.

5 Pile the mixture on to the cooled pastry base, and spread evenly, leaving 1cm (½ inch) clear around the edge. Brush this border with the egg and water glaze.

6 On a lightly floured surface, roll out the remaining pastry into a blanket, large enough to cover the mixture and the base. Put the blanket in place and gently press around the edges to form a seal. Mark this edge with a fork if desired before brushing the whole pie with egg glaze.

7 Return the pie to the oven for 15–20 minutes until the pastry is crisp and golden brown. Serve warm or cold.

Caramelised Onion, Sun-dried Pepper, Tomato and Caper Pie

25g (1 oz) butter
1 tablespoon olive oil
1 large onion, sliced
1 teaspoon sugar
50g (1¾ oz) sun-dried peppers, cut into strips
4 sun-dried tomatoes, roughly chopped
1 tablespoon capers, roughly chopped
2 plum tomatoes, roughly chopped
salt and black pepper

1 In a frying pan, heat the butter with the olive oil. Add the sliced onion and sprinkle with the sugar. Fry the onion over a low heat until golden and caramelised. This may take up to 30 minutes.

2 Meanwhile, place the sun-dried peppers and tomatoes in a bowl, cover with boiling water and set to one side for 20 minutes.

3 Combine the onion, pepper and tomato with the remaining ingredients and season well. Use to fill the flat pie as in the previous recipe. Bake as above.

Artichoke, Pear and Poppy-seed Pie

1 tablespoon olive oil
1 onion, chopped
140g (5 oz) antipasto artichoke hearts, drained and roughly chopped
2 dessert pears, peeled, cored and sliced
1 tablespoon poppy seeds
1 tablespoon roughly chopped fresh mint
juice of ½ lemon
salt and black pepper

1 In a frying pan, heat the oil, add the onion, and fry for 5 minutes until softened.

2 Transfer to a bowl and stir in the artichoke, pear, poppy seeds and mint. Season well with the lemon juice, salt and pepper and use to fill the flat pie as in the previous recipe. Bake as above.

> ⊗ **The poppy seeds can be replaced by 55g (2 oz) Serrano ham, torn into strips.**

Provençal Buttie

Wraps well. Travels well. Eats well. Perfect for a picnic.

Serves 6–8

1 round flat country loaf, about 400g (14 oz) in weight
balsamic vinegar
virgin olive oil
salt and black pepper
1 garlic clove, crushed

For the filling:
1 yellow pepper
25g (1 oz) sun-dried tomatoes in oil
85g (3 oz) antipasto artichokes, sliced
14 Greek black olives, pitted
100g (3½ oz) mozzarella cheese, sliced
1 large ripe avocado, peeled, stoned and sliced

1 Preheat the grill.
2 Cut the pepper in half, remove the core and seeds, and place under the grill. Grill for 5–10 minutes, until the skin blackens and begins to blister. Remove the pepper from the grill and place in a plastic bag. Set to one side and leave to cool.
3 Slice the loaf in three, horizontally. Generously sprinkle each slice with a mixture of 2 tablespoons balsamic vinegar and 3 tablespoons olive oil, and season with salt, black pepper and garlic.
4 Peel the skin from the pepper and cut into strips. Scatter each slice of bread with the pepper strips and other filling ingredients. Drizzle over a little extra olive oil and balsamic vinegar and reassemble the loaf.
5 Press the layers well together and wrap the loaf tightly, in foil or clingfilm. Leave in a cool place for at least 2 hours before serving, cut into cake-like wedges.

Sugar-snap Pea Tart with Ginger Pistou

An intense, savoury tart with a Thai-based dressing.
Perfect for a celebration bash.

Serves 10–12

450g (1 lb) shortcrust pastry
350g (12 oz) sugar-snap peas
10cm (4 inch) piece of fresh root ginger, peeled and roughly chopped
1 large bunch of fresh flat-leaf parsley
2 tablespoons cold-pressed sunflower oil
2 eggs
2 egg yolks
325ml (11 fl oz) crème fraîche
salt and black pepper

For the vinaigrette:
6 tablespoons sweet sherry
1 tablespoon chopped fresh lemongrass
2 garlic cloves, finely chopped
2 fresh red chillies, de-seeded and finely chopped
4 tablespoons dark soy sauce
2 kaffir lime leaves (optional)
1 large fresh basil sprig
juice of 1 lime
6 tablespoons cold-pressed sunflower oil
1 tablespoon fresh basil leaves, roughly chopped

1 Preheat the oven to 200°C/400°F/Gas Mark 6.

2 On a lightly floured surface, roll out the pastry and use to line a 25cm (10 inch) loose-bottomed tart tin. Cover and place in the fridge for 15 minutes.

3 Bring a large pan of water to the boil. Plunge in the sugar-snap peas and simmer for 1 minute. Drain the peas and plunge immediately into a bowl of cold water to cool. Drain well and set to one side.

4 Line the pastry tart case with greaseproof paper and fill with baking beans. Bake in the preheated oven for 10–15 minutes. Remove the greaseproof paper and beans and return the tart case to the oven for a further 3–5 minutes until it is just cooked. Remove from the oven. Reduce the oven temperature to 180°C/350°F/Gas Mark 4.

5 In a small food processor, blend the ginger with the parsley and sunflower oil. Spread over the base of the tart case.

6 Using a small, sharp knife, cut the sugar-snap peas in half by slicing vertically down their length. Scatter the peas over the top of the ginger pistou.

7 In a bowl combine the eggs and egg yolks with the *crème fraîche*, and season with salt and pepper. Pour into the tart case.

8 Return the tart to the oven for 30–35 minutes or until the filling is just set.

9 For the vinaigrette, in a small saucepan gently simmer the sherry, lemongrass, garlic, chilli, soy sauce, lime leaves and basil sprig for 2 minutes. Remove from the heat and combine with the remaining vinaigrette ingredients, seasoning with a little black pepper.

10 To serve, place a portion of tart on each plate with a spoonful of vinaigrette. Serve warm or cold.

ⓧ **Replace the sugar-snap peas with 350g (12 oz) white crab meat at stage 6.**

Hot Brie and Apple Tart

On page 132, we used cheese in the pastry for a sweet apple pie. Here the emphasis is changed and hot Brie is cooked with slices of apple to make a savoury cheese pie. Serve with Cranberry Salsa (see page 16).

Serves 4–6

375g (12 oz) puff pastry
225g (8 oz) Brie, sliced
1 large dessert apple, cored and sliced
black pepper
2 teaspoons clear honey
1 tablespoon fresh thyme leaves
1 egg, beaten

1 Preheat the oven to 220°C/425°F/Gas Mark 7.

2 On a clear, floured surface, roll out the puff pastry into a rectangle 30 × 23cm (12 × 9 inches). Place on a baking sheet and, using a sharp knife, etch in a border 4cm (1½ inches) wide, as if cutting a picture frame, taking care to only cut halfway through the pastry layer. Using a fork, prick the pastry liberally *inside* the border. Place in the fridge and leave to relax for at least 10 minutes.

3 Arrange the sliced Brie inside the pastry border and top with the sliced apple. Season with black pepper.

4 In a small saucepan, gently heat the honey and drizzle it over the apples and Brie. Scatter with the thyme leaves.

5 Glaze the border with beaten egg and bake the tart in the preheated oven for 15–20 minutes until the pastry is well puffed and risen, and the cheese is bubbling hot. Serve at once.

Blue Brie with Plum Marmalade

Bubbling plums on melting Brie. Serve with crusty bread,
eaten as a starter or instead of a cheeseboard.

Serves 10–12

900g (2 lb) blue Brie in one piece
black pepper
1 quantity Plum Marmalade (see page 21)

1 Preheat the oven to 200°C/400°F/Gas Mark 6.

2 Place the piece of Brie on a shallow ovenproof serving dish. Season well with black pepper and spoon over the plum marmalade.

3 Place in the preheated oven for 8–12 minutes or until the Brie is warm and softening. Serve at once.

Honeycomb and Cheeses

A whole honeycomb can be expensive, but looks fantastic,
is entirely edible, and is ideal for a party. For a smaller event, honeycomb
can be bought in pieces in a jar. It can also be served as a starter with a
wedge of cheese and warm Walnut Bread (see page 96).

Serves 25

1 large honeycomb
450g (1 lb) ripe Brie
4 × 115g (4 oz) mild goat's cheeses
450g (1 lb) Wensleydale cheese
450g (1 lb) Port Salut cheese
2 large loaves of rustic-style bread
2 packets of oatcakes

1 Lay the honeycomb out next to your cheeseboard and serve with a selection of mild cheeses. Place a basket of crusty bread and oatcakes to one side and serve it all as an alternative to the traditional cheese course. Serve with a fruity chilled white wine.

Big Coleslaw

Inspired while deli shopping in New York. No mayonnaise, the cabbage is coated with a warm thyme dressing, marinated and finished with hazelnuts.

Serves 12–16

1 small white cabbage, thickly sliced
1 small red cabbage, thickly sliced
1 small green cabbage, thickly sliced
1 bunch of spring onions, roughly chopped
1 large red onion, sliced
1 bunch of fresh thyme, roughly chopped
salt and black pepper
100g (3½ oz) hazelnuts, roasted

For the dressing:
150ml (5 fl oz) cloudy apple juice
85ml (3 fl oz) olive oil
50ml (2 fl oz) cider vinegar
1 teaspoon grainy mustard

1 In a very large bowl, toss together the cabbages, spring onion, red onion and three-quarters of the thyme. Season very well.
2 In a small saucepan, gently heat all the dressing ingredients together and season well with salt and pepper. Pour the warm dressing over the cabbage and onions and toss together well. Cover and refrigerate overnight.
3 To serve, toss the roasted hazelnuts into the cabbage mixture, then turn into a serving dish. Scatter with the remaining thyme, and serve at once.

Crisp Vegetable Black Bean Strudel

*Black bean sauce can now be bought fresh from chill cabinets.
If using normal jarred sauce, use less, as it tends to be stronger.*

Serves 4–6

1 leek, shredded
200g (7 oz) mange tout
3 carrots, peeled and cut into fine strips
225g (8 oz) broccoli florets
115g (4 oz) beansprouts
4 tablespoons fresh black bean sauce
salt and black pepper
4 large filo pastry sheets
sunflower oil
2 teaspoons sesame oil

1 Preheat the oven to 200°C/400°F/Gas Mark 6.

2 Into a pan of boiling water plunge the leek, mange tout, carrot and broccoli. Simmer for 30 seconds, before draining and plunging immediately into cold water. Drain well.

3 In a mixing bowl, combine the blanched vegetables with the beansprouts and black bean sauce. Season with salt and pepper, and set to one side.

4 On a clean tea towel lay one sheet of filo pastry and brush with a little sunflower oil. Lay a second sheet of filo, slightly overlapping the first and brush again. Lay the remaining two sheets on the top in a similar manner.

5 Scatter the vegetables over the filo and spread out. Using the tea towel, roll up into a strudel shape and roll on to a non-stick baking tray. Brush the strudel with a little more sunflower oil and bake in the preheated oven for 25–30 minutes until golden brown.

6 Meanwhile combine the sesame oil with 2 teaspoons sunflower oil. Remove the cooked strudel from the oven, brush with the mixed oil and serve at once, accompanied by some Sesame and Cucumber Pickle (see page 22), if you like.

> Ⓥ **The broccoli florets can be replaced by 1 large duck breast, skinned. Cut the duck into very thin strips and stir-fry in 2 teaspoons grapeseed oil for 2 minutes, before combining with the remaining ingredients at stage 3.**

Alpine Pasta

Pasta, potatoes and cabbage. Here we have Eastern Europe meeting the Med, with an extremely good result.

Serves 6–8

450g (1 lb) red-skinned potatoes, scrubbed and cut into 2.5cm (1 inch) cubes
425ml (15 fl oz) double cream
300ml (10 fl oz) Root Vegetable Stock (see page 29), or stock made with a cube
85g (3 oz) Parmesan cheese, grated
black pepper
1 tablespoon olive oil
225g (8 oz) baby kale, spinach or spring greens
1 garlic clove, crushed
175g (6 oz) feta cheese, cut into cubes
8 fresh lasagne sheets, soaked for 5 minutes in boiling water and drained
freshly grated nutmeg

1 Preheat the oven to 200°C/400°F/Gas Mark 6.

2 In a large saucepan of boiling water, cook the potato pieces until just tender.

3 Place the cream and stock in a pan, bring to the boil and simmer for 2 minutes. Stir in the Parmesan, and season with black pepper.

4 In a frying pan, heat the olive oil, add the kale and garlic, and stir-fry for 1 minute, until just wilted.

5 Now layer up the alpine pasta. Place half of the kale in the base of a large, shallow ovenproof serving dish. Top with half of the potatoes, then half the feta cubes. Pour over a third of the Parmesan sauce. Top the sauce with four sheets of lasagne and another third of the sauce. Repeat with the remaining kale, potato, feta and lasagne, and finish with the remaining sauce. Grind over some black pepper and sprinkle with freshly grated nutmeg.

6 Bake in the oven for 30–35 minutes until golden brown. Serve hot with a crisp salad and crusty bread.

> ⓥ **Replace the feta cheese with 225g (8 oz) garlic sausage, roughly chopped, at stage 5.**

Barley Haggis with Apples and Chestnuts

A tasty version of a traditional, savoury, festive pudding.

Serves 6

sunflower oil
1 tablespoon olive oil
1 large onion, peeled and chopped
2 large carrots, peeled and grated
1 × 290g (10¼ oz) jar of antipasto mushrooms, drained
1 × 215g (7½ oz) can of kidney beans, drained and rinsed
1 × 425g (15 oz) can of green lentils, drained and rinsed
55g (2 oz) pearl barley, cooked
55g (2 oz) porridge oats
2 teaspoons yeast extract or vegetable extract
1 egg
salt and black pepper

For the sauce:
40g (1½ oz) unsalted butter
3 Coxes apples, cored and cut into wedges
a pinch of sugar
240g (8½ oz) whole peeled chestnuts
200ml (7 fl oz) medium-sweet cider
1 tablespoon grainy mustard

1 Prepare a steamer for the haggis. Lightly grease a 1 litre (1¾ pint) pudding basin with a little sunflower oil and line the base with a piece of greaseproof paper.

2 In a saucepan, heat the olive oil and gently fry the onion until golden brown. Add the carrot and mushrooms and fry for a further 3 minutes.

3 Turn this mixture into a large mixing bowl and add the rest of the haggis ingredients. Using a potato masher or fork, mash all the ingredients together. Season well with salt and pepper.

4 Put the haggis mixture into the prepared pudding basin, cover with a double layer of aluminium foil and secure with string.

5 Place in the steamer and cook for 2 hours.

6 About 15 minutes before serving, prepare the sauce. In a small frying pan, melt the butter and fry the apple wedges and sugar for 5 minutes or until just tender. Add the chestnuts, cider and mustard and simmer for 1–2 minutes. Season well with salt and pepper.

7 To serve, remove the haggis from the steamer. Take off the foil and turn the haggis on to a serving plate. Spoon over the apple and chestnuts and trickle over any remaining juices (or hand separately).

Hot Ploughman's Dip

A 1970s fondue brought up to date, a hot crudité! Serve with sticks of crisp celery, spring onions and chunks of warm Walnut Bread (see page 96) for dipping.

Serves 8–10

600ml (1 pint) medium cider
1 bay leaf
225g (8 oz) mature Cheddar cheese, grated
225g (8 oz) Gruyère cheese, grated
4 level teaspoons cornflour
4 tablespoons brandy
black pepper

1 Place the cider and bay leaf in a medium pan and bring to the boil. Simmer for 3 minutes.

2 Add the cheeses and stir until melted.

3 In a bowl, dissolve the cornflour in the brandy. Stir into the cheese sauce. Simmer gently for a further 1–2 minutes and season with black pepper.

4 To serve, take the hot saucepan to the table, arm your guests with napkins and forks and offer them the accompaniments for dipping.

Whiskied Pudding

This boozy pudding makes a great, lighter alternative to the traditional Christmas pudding.

Serves 8

sunflower oil
115g (4 oz) butter
115g (4 oz) soft brown sugar
2 eggs
1 tablespoon plain flour
225g (8 oz) fresh granary breadcrumbs
1 teaspoon ground cinnamon
juice and grated rind of 1 orange
225g (8 oz) dried apricots, chopped
115g (4 oz) sultanas
115g (4 oz) raisins
1 carrot, peeled and grated
4 tablespoons whisky

1 Lightly oil a 1.2 litre (2 pint) pudding basin and place a piece of greaseproof paper in the bottom.

2 In a large bowl, cream together the butter and sugar. Beat in the eggs and stir in the flour and breadcrumbs.

3 Add the cinnamon, orange juice and rind, apricots, sultanas, raisins, carrot and half the whisky. Mix together thoroughly.

4 Cover and steam the pudding for 2 hours (see page 154).

5 Allow the pudding to stand for 15 minutes before turning out. Flame with the remaining whisky and serve with custard or ice-cream.

Pashka

Pashka means Easter in Russian. A traditional pashka is shaped in a four-sided wooden container. For this recipe you can use a flower pot or plastic flower pot lined with muslin or a J-cloth: use one which has about a 1.4 litre (2½ pint) capacity.

Serves 8–10

675g (1½ lb) curd cheese
100g (3½ oz) blanched almonds, chopped
200g (7 oz) bitter plain chocolate, chopped
3 teaspoons vanilla extract
85g (3 oz) raisins
2 egg yolks
85g (3 oz) caster sugar
115g (4 oz) unsalted butter, softened
150ml (5 fl oz) double cream

For the sauce:
500g (1 lb 2 oz) fresh red summer fruits, or frozen, thawed
2–3 tablespoons icing sugar, or to taste
1 tablespoon brandy

1 In a large mixing bowl combine the cheese, almonds, chocolate, vanilla and raisins together.
2 In a small bowl cream the egg yolks with the sugar until light and creamy. Beat in the butter and cream and add to the cheese mixture.
3 Pour the mixture into the prepared mould. Fold the excess muslin over the top, cover with a plate, and weigh the plate down with anything heavy (i.e. a can of beans). Chill the pashka for at least 12 hours, standing the pot on a dish so that any excess liquid drains away.
4 To serve, place all the sauce ingredients in a saucepan. Heat gently until warmed through. Turn the pashka out into the centre of a large serving dish and spoon over the berry sauce. Serve at once.

Amaretti Berries

Cream tea, berry-style, with Amaretti. This no-cook, no-fuss, self-service pudding – which I was served at a friend's – has now become a firm favourite in my household.

Serves 8

900g (2 lb) mixed berries (strawberries, blackberries, raspberries, blackcurrants and redcurrants)
1 packet of butter shortbread biscuits
600ml (1 pint) extra-thick double cream
1 bottle of Amaretti liqueur

1 Pile the berries on to a large serving platter.

2 Preheat the oven to 190°C/375°F/Gas Mark 5. Warm the shortbread biscuits for 5 minutes in the oven.

3 Take the berries, shortbread, cream and Amaretti liqueur to the table and allow your guests to serve themselves. Spoon some berries into a dessert bowl, sprinkle with a generous amount of Amaretti liqueur, top with a spoonful of cream and eat with a piece of warmed shortbread.

Index